Just Cats cannot fail to give considerable pleasure to all who are interested in cats, whether owners or simply admirers. Entertaining and highly readable, spiced with stories and anecdotes about individual cats, it makes an outstandingly good gift book; and it is also a first class manual of advice for the cat owner, covering every breed and all aspects of caring for and breeding cats.

Fernand Méry, an internationally acknowledged authority on cats, draws from his great knowledge of the subject with lucidity, wit and an engagingly light touch.

JUST CATS

Ϙ ——————————————————————

FERNAND MÉRY

translated by
John Rosenberg & Elizabeth King

QUARTET BOOKS   LONDON

Published by Quartet Books Limited 1973
27 Goodge Street, London W1P IFD

First published in Great Britain by Souvenir Press Ltd., 1957

Copyright © 1957 by Dr Fernand Méry

ISBN 0 704 31037 6

Printed in Great Britain by
Hunt Barnard Printing Ltd., Aylesbury, Bucks.

PREFACE

A book about the cat? After so many others?
After all the immortal works celebrating him? After Moncriff
the cat's biographer? Baudelaire his confidante? Colette his
accomplice?

Why not? In a century where every hour sees some change,
every minute a discovery, one need not worry that everything
has been said and that one is too late. An entire unknown world
is still before us; the world of animals, of which we know
almost nothing.

Cuvier, from his ivory tower, uttered this absurd pronounce-
ment one day: 'There is not a single living mammal which is
unknown to Science.' Six months later, one of his colleagues
discovered the Indian tapir, and modern specialists have
discovered the okapi. Who can say if there are not other
animals still unknown in the unexplored parts of Australia,
Antarctica or America?

Nor could anyone maintain that we are in possession of all
the facts about the known animals. Every day, somewhere, a
bit of light is shed on the mystery. Someone discovers that
most carnivores are sensitive to supersonic waves, that the
bat is a kind of radar, that the gregarious insects have a secret
code: the glow-worm giving an optical signal and the ants and

bees needing no guide to any place to which they are directed by one of their kind.

If the vanished type of the above-mentioned famous zoologist could come back to earth today, he would be thoroughly discomfited, his pretensions and ignorance brought home to him.

Each generation contributes something – errors or truth – to the world's store of knowledge. It is far from my intention, certainly, to try to reconsider the opinions or talents of those who have studied and celebrated the cat in the course of centuries. But today we have laboratories which disclose radioactivity, measure chromosomes and show the balance of hormones. The slow-motion camera, the telescopic lens, the electronic microscope, reveal the animal world, which was previously inaccessible.

A new book on the cat? Why not, if it is to contribute to the reinstatement of a creature who has been treated unjustly because he is still the most secret and solitary in the world. To his mystery is allied his martyrdom.

What are his origins?

What is he?

What will be his evolution?

I shall try to throw some light on these obscure points, by citing legend, history, anecdote, observation, psychology and experimental research in turn.

It seems to me that the cat, fabulous creature that he is, neither tamed nor savage, with his power of inspiring fear and love, and his terrible history of suffering – the cat, it seems, might well be grateful for any contribution towards understanding and knowledge of him.

F.M.

I

The Origins of the Cat

1. FROM LEGEND
TO HISTORY

The origins of the cat? If one is to believe the tradition handed down in the Orient, one must go back to the Flood! Mulla, once ambassador of the Sublime Porte, wrote:

The Ark had already been afloat for several weeks, when one morning the pig, that lackey, scratched himself and spewed forth a couple of rats – such prolific rats that Noah, after having supplicated God, called the lion to his aid. The lion stretched, roared in the pig's face, and blew his nose so violently that a cat sprang out of his nostrils – such a quarrelsome cat as to fall on the rats and kill them without further ado. Only one couple escaped with their lives: and from that day the cat was so arrogant that Noah, to punish him, tied him up on the bridge when the storm was at its height. It is from this that so many cats get their disdainful expression and that horror of water which still pursues them.

Other sources would have it that the cat was 'the offspring of favours bestowed by a lioness on her husband's court jester, an enterprising monkey who had made the lion laugh'.

Fortunately, as credulous people see resemblances everywhere, legends are not history.

What has history, then, to say on the subject? What of all

the documents of sculpture, painting, engraving and writing that have come down to us?

Who were the first discoverers of the cat?

The Mohicans, in Professor Hoyle's view: those primitive Indians who later, in the Andes, created Inca civilization. This scholarly Peruvian, director of Trujillo's Archaeological Museum, showed through the analysis of very ancient pottery that the cat was the supreme divinity of the Mohicans. Portrayed with the face of a shepherd or musician, doctor or soldier, the cat on these relics always has the look of a human being. Muzzle extended, whiskers bristling and claws well in evidence, he is accompanied or preceded by a dog; and both trample a human-looking lizard which, lowly, servile and fawning, symbolizes the unenlightened people.

In subsequent ages? There is, of course, Egypt.

The significant history of the cat begins only with Egypt, although only one point here is generally agreed on: it was during the Fifth Dynasty – not the Twelfth (as Champfleury held) or the Eighteenth – that a small and unknown feline was taken into the Egyptian temples, replacing the ravenous lions which had hitherto guarded the entrances. This dating was proved when the reproduction of a cat in a large collar was brought to light in the tomb of Ti.

One wonders where these cats, not to be found on earlier hypogea or sculptures, came from. They may have been utilized first by the Nubians. But this detail is of little importance, since chronologically Nubia and Ancient Egypt are almost one.

Before Egypt?

Before, one might venture to surmise, the cat most probably lived in a savage state in Africa. At all events, the African has always had a certain regard for cats, or at any rate tolerated their presence. He doesn't pet them, cosset them, or feed them; and yet certain black peoples who eat monkey or dog meat and even, from time to time, leg of man, will go hungry in preference to eating a cat. This may well be an inheritance from the time when these coloured peoples were the soldiers or servants

4

of the Pharaohs. In Egypt they must have seen the cat at work against the great pestilence, the rat. They must have seen how cats were heaped with honours. And from this it came about, whether through tradition or wonder or fear, that the African of today likes cats.

But, again, what of the cat before the time of the Pharaohs?

Certainly there have been quite widespread discoveries of bones of cats mixed with those of dogs, horses or oxen of the Stone Age: there is no doubt that wildcats – and small game, too, for that matter – existed then.

However, all authorities agree on this point: *the domestic cat is not a descendant of the wildcat.* Every time attempts have been made to cross-breed the two species, to couple wild and domestic cats, the results have been most disappointing. The domestic cat can be mated with the wild cat of the jungle, with the Asiatic cat and even with the lynx; but the offspring of these difficult marriages usually die very young, and the experiment can never survive the first generation.

Certainly we are better informed about the mammoth, the wild ox, or the cave-dwelling tiger than we are about the domestic cat of pre-Egyptian times. Could this be because before that time the domestic cat was simply non-existent?

A PANTHER GONE WRONG?

It is clear that we have no exact evidence on this subject. Traces of the feline species have been found everywhere. Apart from Australia, Madagascar, the West Indies and the polar regions, it existed everywhere, from the earliest appearance of mammals on the earth.

But, the lynx excepted, the Old and New Worlds have not a single feline type in common – not a single type of all the many.

America has the puma (resembling a lion), the jaguar (something like the panther) and the ocelot (not unlike a small leopard); but there are neither real lions nor real tigers in the New World. Among the smaller felines there are none – not the margay (a striped feline of the South), nor the eyra (a cat of the pampas), nor the colocolo (reminiscent of the lynx) – that could really be used to prove the ordinary cat's heredity. The domestic cats of America are immigrants, and not indigenous.

Then, where did they come from?

Asia? Could they be descendants of the mottled cats of the Sunda Isles or of the Bengal cats? Or of the ones from Java or Sumatra? Or of the red-brown or 'ornamented' ones of the Indies?

Or they might originally have come from Africa. From the kaffir cats of the equator, the black-footed species of the south, the puss-in-boots of North Africa, or the Sudanese 'gloved' cat.

Then there are as possible ancestors caracals and servals, found pretty well throughout Africa: the former of an even colouring, darker at the ears; the latter more or less striped.

Like the cat, both the serval and the caracal have thirty teeth; and either might have evolved the domestic cat of Egypt. But caracals are never striped, and servals are never plainly coloured. There is no small feline type which could have fathered that strain of such infinite variety: Siameses, Spanish tri-coloured cats, blue-grey cats, Abyssinians, white cats and all-black cats.

However, there remains one savage feline, a big one, which has so many points in common with the cat family that it is tempting here to advance an opinion, albeit cautiously and suppositiously, on the origins of the cat – while noting certain anatomical differences (in regard to the brain particularly).

Felis pardus, the panther of Africa, is, as aptly described by Professor Bertin, a *super-cat*. On a larger scale, it has the same features, the beauty, the gracefulness, strength and suppleness; and, what is even more significant, it varies, like the cat, in form and colour according to the climate and habitat, without it being possible to group panthers into different species.

With the panther, as with the cat, one never finds two coats identical. And the panther, like the cat, is found in almost every climate. In Africa, near the Mediterranean as well as the

Cape and in the heart of Central Africa. In Asia, from Japan to Asia Minor, and from the Sunda Isles to the south of Siberia.

If one of the varieties, the panther nebulose, with its splendid grey, irregularly marked coat, could fail to remind one of a cat, another, the black Javanese panther, when it crouches ready to spring, its tail beating the air nervously, is the super-cat *par excellence*. This black panther never has a uniform colouring, as one might imagine, but is always, like the cat, more or less ringed with faint marks.

By studying Egyptian mummified cats Cuvier thought it possible to prove that the species is immutable. On the other hand, Darwin, by taking a cat to Paraguay, proved how little change is needed to alter an animal to the point of giving it a new form.

Can this be the answer, then? An abrupt mutation? The sudden appearance of an arbitrary form of dwarfishness in a species of African panther affected by some little-known phenomena? A mutation which, becoming hereditary, gave rise to the cat, to be gradually tamed and domesticated by the Nubians and the Egyptians?

This theory would be tempting indeed but for one detail: the difference in the pupillary opening, round in all other felines and oval in the cat. However, we may note, that famous pupillary crack is not altogether special to the one genus: it is also found in the civet-cat, a pleasant creature which is readily domesticated – like a cat!

EGYPT, PARADISE OF CATS

What do we know of ancient Egypt, a shadowy country beginning at Karnak in the midst of the temples of Thebes and reaching its apotheosis in the sombre tombs of the Valley of Kings? The gods, with human bodies and animal heads, expressed by their strange form the limitations of a world to which the minds of mere men had no access.

Egypt is the logical background in which to search for a trace, a detail, that may help the researcher in his delvings into the history of the civilized cat.

I have visited the remains of Ancient Egypt. The most vivid reproductions of cats are on the tomb of the sculptors Apuki and Nebamun at Thebes and date from the reign of Amenophis III; also in the temple of Medineth-Abou, on the bas-reliefs dedicated to hunting. In these the cats are represented as taller, larger and with longer lines than our most highly-bred Siameses of today, and more often than not are on leads for hunting the aquatic marsh-birds for their masters.

Were they brown or black? Uniformly coloured or spotted? Ringed or striped?— these cats, so highly prized that their masters went into mourning when one of them died. Indeed, the killing of these cats was punishable by death. They were so much admired that from Memphis to Thebes the most sought-after women, the most successful courtesans, were those whose eyes had the colour and shape of a cat's, and whose figure and bearing had a cat's suppleness.

We cannot, of course, be certain about the simple facts of the appearance of these cats.

There exists at the British Museum a painting from Thebes, in which the cat is represented as a somewhat irregularly striped tiger; but there have also come down to us pictures of cats on papyrus, where the animal, coloured evenly, is just slightly marked with streaks halfway up the paws and a third of the way along the tail. The cats of Bubastis, of Hahbe Antar, of Arthemidos, have shed no further light on this problem.

Scarcely sixty years ago, a discovery was made in Central Egypt, at Beni Hassan, of an actual cemetery where 300,000 embalmed and mummified cats had been sleeping for thousands of years.

No archaeologist was on the spot to prevent the inevitable vandalism; stupidly the graveyard was destroyed – an irreparable loss. It would have been enough to have kept just a random hundred of these cats for us to know now what the colouring and texture of the hair of these first cats were. By taking an average, we should have gained an approximate idea of their size.

By a wild combination of circumstances, this mass of cats was thrown into the hold of a ship departing for England – later to be sold as manure! Professor W. M. Conway, in the

English Illustrated Magazine of the time, wrote down all the details of this unpardonable crime. Twenty tons of Egyptian cats in an admirable state of preservation were transported to Liverpool, and almost all sold to farmers at £4 per ton, to be mixed into the English soil as though they were mere dung.

Undoubtedly there are in existence some damaged or half-destroyed mummies, the scientific value of which is not realized. It can only be hoped that one day some interested specialist may be able to buy and study them, so throwing some light on the question. Before the 1914 war, Dr Ehrenburg and an anatomist, de Blainville, tried in vain. After performing autopsies on several mummified cats and analysing the kind of cloths in which they were bound, etc., they concluded that these were Abyssinian cats. At Cairo we found only one tomb, an empty sarcophagus of stone: that of a cat commemorated by its master, the chief of the Order of Architects, who had his own name engraved in his companion's epitaph.

When one considers that an entire city, situated between the branches of the Nile off the present-day Benha-el-Asl on the railway line from Ismailia to Cairo, was once dedicated to cats, one is surprised to learn that today cats are rare in Egypt. Certainly one sees memorials of them everywhere, but often confused with the various effigies of other, indeterminate felines.

Is it a cat or a lion, that overwhelming statue of Sekmet with the splendid body of a woman, which leaps out from its obscure background? For counterpart it has Bastet, a milder but equally disturbing figure. The one is terrifying, the other on the surface reassuring; but the dividing line is not quite clear between the savage beast and the charming little cat.

Elsewhere we find the same confusion between goats and rams, jackals and wolves, wolves and dogs even. And as Ancient Egypt has left no document comparable to the Bible or the Koran, there is nowhere to trace exact information or references.

Only those statues which are completely, in both head and body, of cats can help to give a picture of the Ancient Egyptian domestic cat. All proportions being similar, this type of the statues resembles that most friendly and tameable feline: the cheetah. Aesthetically only the cheetah – if it had retractile claws, that is – is the counterpart of these statues. The lion or the tiger, with their larger, flatter muzzles, never had that loose frame, those paws with long and solid toes, that comparatively narrow chest between very straight shoulders, and that serpentine head.

But Ancient Egypt was only yesterday, comparatively speaking. What after all are two or three thousand years in the evolution of a species? The domestic cat seems a comparative newcomer, when one considers that the dog has been man's companion since our first ancestors so many hundreds of thousands of years ago.

All we know is that from his first appearance in Ancient Egypt the cat became a veritable godhead, the sacred host in all his glory. A male cat was held to be the ally of the sun and the scourge of Apopi, serpent of night. A female was beloved of the common people and regarded as a Lady of Heaven.

This astonishing ascendancy lasted for nearly a thousand years, up to the period of decadence, the collapse of the dynasty of the Pharaohs, and the birth of the Christian religion. The new Faith cast a dazzling enlightenment, but consigned the cat to perpetual darkness and the most tragic of destinies.

GREATNESS AND DECLINE

With the advent of Christianity, in a moment, as it were, the cat was no longer of the world of the living. There is only one Scriptural allusion to the cat: in the Book of Baruch (Ch. VI, 20–1),[1] more specifically in the epistle of Jeremias warning the Jews against idolatry in their captivity in Babylon. The prophet describes the Babylonian idols as blackened with smoke and crawling with owls and cats.

No sacred text spoke of the cat. The usurper and every reminder of him was condemned. Condemned perhaps for the very reason that his origins and what he is were completely unknown; and such a riddle, coupled with the fact of his recent divinity, could not be suffered to trouble the Christian spirit.

[1] The reference is to the Vulgate.

By a strange coincidence, the dog, hitherto despised and hounded as the most accused and impure of beasts, was to have an unlooked-for restitution with the coming of the Redeemer.

With his aura of fidelity, goodness and obedience, the dog was to win back the role which since time immemorial had been his in relation to man: the role of hunting companion, housemate, protector and friend.

It must not be imagined that the cat, being a sacred animal, had a purely non-functional cult in Egyptian life. For all that he was a demi-god, the cat destroyed serpents, hunted rats, kept guard on the house, and followed his master to the marshes, where he started game. In other words, he took the dog's place.

And yet the dog existed in Egypt. Researchers have found the odd greyhound or dachshund engraved or painted on those rare documents, a dagger handle or the fragments of a vase. So Egypt made use of the dog, but made little of him too. He was even deprived of his last office, since Anubis, god of death, was not a dog but a jackal.

FROM EPILEPSY TO CHRISTIANITY

The question arises why the dog, who from man's first appearance had shared in his stumbling efforts, should have yielded his place to the cat in Egypt. Why did the cat suddenly assume such great importance, to hold the place of honour in this civilized people's daily life for almost four thousand years, in preference to the tried and trusted dog? This problem has never been considered.

Here we must presume to touch on a corner of medicine. In those days princes and Pharaohs, consanguineous as they were, often suffered from a strange illness known to us as epilepsy. This 'High Illness', probably so-called because it attacked the nobles, was rarely fatal. The symptoms of the crisis resembled those of hydrophobia. But the true hydrophobia, contracted through a bite or contact with infected saliva, was invariably fatal. So is it any wonder that the priests, the courtesans, trepanners, embalmers, merchants, all those who gravitated about the throne – confusing the two diseases – bothered about the risk and took every possible precaution?

'Perhaps by the privilege of birth,' they might have told themselves, 'princes and kings are protected against this illness being fatal – but we aren't.'

So it followed that the dog was declared to be impure and was denied access to the places – palaces, villas, temples – where all other creatures, from the hawk to the crocodile, were allowed.

However it was, when Egypt collapsed the Church passed a death-sentence on the cat and gave the dog his revenge. The dog, as privileged animal of the hunt, was to have the right of entry into churches till the day when the severe Charlemagne, by the terms of the Third Capitularies, forbade the wild young nobles to take their packs of hounds into holy places. From this arose the tradition of blessing dogs on the parvis.

The dog reinstated, the cat, being a loathed reminder of paganism, was relegated to the shades.

NEITHER GREECE NOR ROME
UNDERSTOOD THE CAT

We shall have to go back to Egypt later: it is our chief source, just as one goes back to Greece and Rome in trying to understand man, his ambition and vicissitudes. Continuing the history of the cat, let us turn to Greece.

If Herodotus is to be believed, the Egyptians accused the Greeks of the theft over centuries not only of their sciences, their astronomy, philosophy, geometry and so on, but also of their cats.

The Greeks had discovered the Egyptians' prime secret for preserving their crops. In turn, they had tried to breed small carnivorous animals to destroy the pestilential mice. But this attempt had to be abandoned rather quickly, as the weasels killed goats, sucked the blood of chickens, and bothered with mice only when the fighting spirit took them.

How then to get hold of cats, which the Egyptians prized so

highly as to forbid their export, as well as devoting a cult to them? The only way was to steal them. The Greeks set about this, with unequal success. Centuries passed in a patient coming and going of Greek spies bent on stealing the cats of Luxor or Thebes; and in turn Egyptian agents were despatched to recover the invaluable property, in the interests of the State as well as of the Supreme Faith.

'Alexander the Great,' said Margaret Cooper, who described this strange contest, 'like all conquerors, abhorred cats. Was it to exterminate them that in 332 B.C. he conquered Egypt? However it was, the cats emerged as the winners, and the conquest had no lasting duration.'

As for Rome, despite the writings of Pliny, Cicero and Aristotle, and although certain troops chose the cat as their mascot (the *felices seniores,* the territorials of that time, had a red cat on a vermilion background on the standard of their legion), Rome had no more understanding of the cat than she had of the dog.

It was a cat, however, who caused the spark that set off the war between Rome and Egypt. When a Roman citizen living in Egypt accidentally killed a cat, the King himself tried to protect the man, but in vain. The enraged people seized the Roman, stoned him to death, and offered his mutilated body to the outraged shade of the sacred animal.

Hostilities began, and ended only with the deaths of Mark Antony and Cleopatra, when Egypt became a Roman province and the cat an untouchable.

Whether the anecdote is real or apocryphal, it at least indicates the position of the cat in history.

INDIA, CHINA AND JAPAN

It cannot be surprising to learn that the cat was sanctified in a similar way by the Hindus. True believers are still obliged, as laid down in orthodox Hindu teaching, to shelter at least one cat under each roof.

The cat (who was to reach Persia by the beginning of the fifth century) penetrated into China in the year 1000 B.C., and

13

from China on to Japan, where mice were destroying the silk-worms and imperilling this industry, which already was prosperous.

Immediately the cat met, among these Far Eastern peoples who in so many ways resembed him, a natural sympathy, as well as a blind confidence, naïve and tender, illustrated by the following story:[1]

In the year 999, in the tenth day of the Fifth Moon, at the Imperial Palace of Kyoto, a cat gave birth for the first time recorded here, and to five little kittens. The Emperor so marvelled at this that he charged his ministers with the care of them; they were to bring the kittens up in exactly the same way as they had been nursed as children. When the kittens were grown, he made it known at Court that he wished the breeding to continue.

The power of cats over people who fall under their sway is well known. After this the cats multiplied and won the people's hearts; until it became the fashion to cherish them and keep them on leads, to the great joy of the mice, who were no longer frightened of their presence. Then, concerned when the plague of mice increased, the people had images of cats engraved on the houses and even put up statues of cats, imagining that this would be enough to make the mice disappear at once. It was all quite useless, of course; the mice multiplied and the plague of them was worse than ever, on the grain as well as the silkworms.

Not till 1602 did the Government decide on energetic measures. Then the toms were nationalized; it was decreed that they should be set at liberty again; and it was forbidden, under grave penalties, to buy or sell them or even give them as presents.

Liberated, the Japanese cats did their friendly duty by the people: the mice beat a retreat, and the silkworms were left in peace.

[1] V. de Visser: *Chiens et Chats dans le folklore japonais.*

But the work of Margaret Cooper Gay,[1] revealing the humorous as well as the factual aspect of the history of cats in Europe, is even more exact in its detail.

Do you know the reason for the legendary affection which the English have for cats? Because the Scots, it is said, were the first of all nordic peoples to harbour the cat.

Fergus I of Scotland was descended from General Galsthelus, the Greek commander-in-chief of the Egyptian Army at the time when Moses delivered the children of Israel into safety. His army wiped out in the Red Sea, Galsthelus managed to escape, with his wife as well as his possessions. The wife, Scota, was Pharaoh's daughter; but she did not hesitate to follow her husband to a European coast later to become Portugal. There they founded a kingdom, the kingdom of Brigantium.

More than a thousand years later Fergus, their descendant, moved northwards and became king of an island to which he gave the pleasing name of Scota, his ancestress. Scotland was created; and Fergus introduced into the Highlands the sons, many generations removed, of those adored cats which his ancestress had taken with her from the Nile.

'The mighty but amiable cat, pride of the household,' was to conquer England as he had conquered the Orient. In Scotland he has become a symbol of courage and fidelity: just as the English speak of a fighter as a 'cock', so the Scots use the word 'cat'.

Need one add that the old clan Cattan has no other origin, that the Earl of Caithness is really the Earl of Cats, just as the Duke of Sutherland is the Duke Cate, and that 'the bagpipes of the ladies from hell still caterwaul like wrathful toms'?

[1] *How to Live with a Cat.*

In the fifth-century writings of Palladius the word 'cat' appears in base Latin under the form of *catus*, an expression borrowed from the Gauls, and of which there are equivalents in Celtic and Gallic.

It was doubtless then that the cat set foot on European soil, first in the Low Countries, where the Romans founded and named a tribe 'Those of the Cats' near the ancient mouth of the Rhine.

Occasionally monks would arrive from Egypt, also bringing cats. This contributed to the budding interest in, if not taste for, the species which the Franks, Celts and Gauls had at the time when the region was overwhelmed by Barbarian hordes, dirty and cruel, bringing ruin and death as they pillaged and burnt everything from Rome to the Rhine. And with them, too, they brought the plague – and the rat, until then unknown in Europe.

There followed dark ages of barbarism, a time when the civilized peoples, fearing epidemics as well as the vandals, kept their cat with them like a precious talisman.

From now on the cat would spread to every part of Europe, from the North Sea to the Adriatic. Countries made laws to protect them. They fetched a price in gold guaranteed by the State, the pride varying according to their weight, strength and valour in ratting. What was more, whoever killed a cat, a real fighter and guardian cat, had to pay a fine in milk, lamb and wool, or a quantity of grain sufficient to cover the entire length of the victim's body when held by the tip of the tail with the head brushing the ground.

Was this to usher in a period of peace and plenty for the cat?

Alas, this pleasant time lasted only until the barbarians from the north discovered the creature's virtues, its grace, beauty and charm. More than a thousand years after the death of Cleopatra, there flourished in Germany the cult of Freya, a strange, orgiastic rite inspired by the cat, its loves, its cries and its combats: a rite which made the cat so important in the hysterical imagination of women that Christianity intervened, and the cat, limb of Satan, agent of the devil, became, *urbi et orbi*, an unclean animal.

And this time of hostility and proscription lasted, in France at least, until the returning Crusaders brought back the Black Death. The dedicated knights returning from the Holy Land did not return alone. Unknowingly they carried certain stowaways in the hold of their ships. They brought back the black rat, which soon overran castle and cottage, until there seemed no way of stopping the pestilence. For better or worse, they set what few cats there were on to the black killer from the East.

These cats were both those which the knights brought from Palestine (to where they had come from Egypt), and those European ones which were ladies' pets, presents from their husbands or lovers.

According to Armand Steens, it was first the ladies in religious orders who took in the cats brought back from the Crusades. By a general rule of these religious communities, the abbesses and nuns were forbidden to own either useful or pet animals; but the cloisters and convents were infected with vermin, so an exception was made in favour of the cat. Those brought by the knights were engaging and handsome, with long muzzles and neat paws; but, far from their native Africa, they grew delicate and suffered from the cold, and the race would have rapidly become extinct had not the queens and toms, acting on some instinct of race-preservation, interbred, in the course of their forays, with common vagrant cats of the woods.

We need look no further for the origins of the two types now predominant: the squat, autochthonous ones, with short paws and round head; and the exotic, long-lined ones. Both strains mingled haphazardly, predominating or counterbalancing to produce the present-day cat.

Noble or common, striped, ringed, tri-coloured or uniformly coloured, the cats rushed to the fray, and in a few months had emerged victorious.

Their praises were sung, they were heaped with laurels; but the danger past, the deliverer was likewise forgotten.

Time passed; and the cats, allowed to rest for twenty years on the love and esteem they had earned, woke up to find themselves literally in the fire.

The Church, her moment of indulgence having passed, now resumed the battle. To these innocent creatures she dedicated the deadliest hatred, the most cruel butchery, that the mind could devise. Hundreds of thousands of them, hunted down in every country, were crucified or burnt alive, thrown howling into the stoves. This was the epoch of auto-da-fés, those unholy bonfires of cats which nobles encouraged and priests presided over. It was the epoch of the sinister fires of St John, where a pole erected within a circle of fire offered brief respite to the agonized creatures: clinging to the pole, they fought one another off until, one by one, they fell back into the blazing hollow of the fire.

To add irony to the situation, there were even quite serious trials of cats, in which these sentences were justified. In the name of nobleness of mind and the fight against vice and scandal, Justice supported the Clergy.

In 1484 Pope Innocent VIII himself took up the struggle, setting out to hound down the friends of cats and, accusing them of sorcery, pronouncing anathema against them. The Inquisition began.

The frenzy knew no bounds. It spread to Germany, to England. By tens of thousands women were executed for protecting, feeding or looking after cats. A hundred years after Cromwell, so-called witches who owned cats were still being burnt alive.

It was hatred, lasting for generations and crossing oceans; a hatred so strong and tenacious that New England alone was to hold over two thousand trials for cat-sorcery.

However . . . though the first chronicles of America rarely mention the cat, it is to a Frenchman, Père Sagard, that the United States owed her first present of one.

Having given a cat to a Huron Indian, the priest imagined that the savage would accord the newcomer the same importance which all civilized peoples in the course of centuries had granted it. But the Indians did not believe in its power. What could this pretty creature possibly accomplish against the hosts of black rats, grey rats, field mice, rabbits and squirrels which ceaselessly plagued them and devoured their crops? They allowed the cats to die out; and not until entire colonies, like Pennsylvania in 1749, were gravely endangered, was it decided, at a price paid in gold, to import cats to America.

If the Indians had had more confidence in that first French missionary they might, thanks to the cat, have become shepherds and farmers through being able to protect their corn; and – who knows? – the entire destiny of the New World might have been changed. But it is as difficult to implant a new idea as to efface, from day to day, the customs or the agonies which have through generations established themselves imperceptibly in the hearts of men.

How many intelligent and enlightened people of today suspect that it is to the hot iron, the *strappado*, the horrors of the Inquisition, that their innermost minds are harking back when instinctively to avert what was once thought to be bad luck, they touch wood because a black cat has crossed the street from left to right? Superstition or unconscious recollection?

CATS AND WAR

With his hopeful and serene philosophy, the Buddhist has always kept a place for the cat. A little-known fact of recent history can show how the Burman values the cat, and what a high place he accords it in man's evolution towards beatitude.

The help that England got from Burma in the last war is owed to the cat. The population, as it happened, was deeply influenced by Japanese propaganda against the building of the famous road that was so strategic and indispensable to the Allies. The labourers fled from the yards, to disappear in the impenetrable forest.

It was then that an English colonel, familiar with the beliefs of the people and the folklore of the country, had the idea of having white cats painted on the trucks, jeeps and road-plans. Meanwhile, the English and American airmen had instructions to collect as many white cats as they could find, and as quickly as possible.

The results were not long in appearing. Swiftly the news circulated in the jungle that the aeroplanes had become the refuge and the favoured abode of the sacred felines. From this the natives concluded at once that the gods favoured the Allies, turning a deaf ear to all Japanese offers.

The English had simply re-enacted Cambyses's classic stratagem before Pelusium in 500 B.C. When the Persians besieged what is now Tisa'a, near Port Said, they had hundreds of cats with them. Rather than risk seeing a single of these creatures killed – so Paul Vosgien related – the Egyptians surrendered.

MAN'S INGRATITUDE

But let us continue down the centuries, returning to Europe, to France and England.

Times changed. Loved by some and hated by others, the cat continued to waver between bondage and a return to liberty. And the rats made capital out of this, returning once again to the attack in 1750, this time in the guise of the terrible sewer rat. For a third time the cats, or what remained of the cats, were called to the rescue.

Belgium had re-established in 1720 an ancient and horrible custom, previously abolished in 1674: the custom of hurling cats from the tops of cathedral towers.

As for Germany, Archbishop Clement of Cologne had in 1747 issued a hunting regulation obliging cat-owners to have the creatures' ears clipped, and imposing a fine of half a florin for every cat found with this not done. Cat-lovers ended by growing weary of breeding, and the creatures themselves seemed stunned into giving up the struggle.

Hunted down, weakened and decimated, they were to become so rare that in the seventeenth century they were listed in the items of inventories, wills and successions.

The sewer rat thrived. Cunning, intelligent, ferocious, it knew how to make its way. Instead of devoting its attention to domestic battles (as its predecessor, the black rat, had done), it attacked in bands and routed the last cats.

Thereafter, comfortably set up in swarming, greedy packs, the sewer rat continued to increase, multiply and invade towns and villages.

The French Revolution and the Empire had other pre-occupations. And Napoleon was on the scene...

In spite of the fact that he drew much of his inspiration from Egypt, Napoleon disliked cats. He preferred to leave his experts to do battle against the rats. But the cleverest attempts of his reign failed: the poisons devised were too dangerous, and the traps over-complicated.

So it was necessary, though it went against the grain, to reinstate the cat, cry up his virtues and encourage him to multiply.

Too late. The rats, ten times more prolific, and secure in their tenure under every roof, in every sewer and in the labyrinth of cellars, scorned these few sleepy cats. This century, too, ended before man, perverse and ungrateful, had saved the cat from his unhappy fate.

THE CAT SANCTIFIED – BY MISTAKE

The age of Pasteur was to follow, the era of great inventions and discoveries: that of microbes, above all. And here a paradox – because of a misapprehension – was to reinstate the cat triumphantly.

When it was known that just a few minute, invisible creatures could undermine the health of a strong man; when it was known that hundreds of microbes could sow disease and bring death to entire cities, there broke out, especially in France, a sudden microphobia.

If the microbe was an animal, a kind of living being which thrived on dirt and lack of hygiene, what risks were not run in consorting with animals, which never cleaned themselves! An instinctive barrier, a kind of wall, was immediately erected between humankind and the animal world.

The Darwinians entered the controversy, speaking of biological fraternity. But the argument went against them. 'If the beasts', it was retorted, 'are so close to man, then they are all the more dangerous because of their very resemblance to him and their familiar contacts.' A wave of zoophobia spread, putting both the horse and the dog out of favour. People would avoid touching a lamb, or approaching too close to a canary, or keeping a turtle. These precautions were carried out to the point of the ridiculous.

It was in such a climate of feeling that veterinary science, in the wake of Pasteur, earned its first distinction. It can hardly be wondered that the prejudice which greeted it then still persists.

And the cat, in this new age of hygiene? Well, the cat, who generally kept himself aloof from other animals; the cat, who passed whole hours in cleaning and washing himself – the cat became overnight, in the eyes of all, the only clean animal, the only one which, it stood to reason, could not transmit microbes, since the cat had vowed an everlasting hatred of rats and mice.

Then, reassured about the cat, and cheated out of having much to do with other animals, people suddenly built up a tremendous enthusiasm for this creature which had been hated and despised for so long.

This apotheosis happened everywhere: painters, sculptors, philosophers, poets set about revealing an unforeseen passion for the cat. Thus, fashion lending a hand, came the pedestal, the consecration, the revenge. The 'limb of the devil' became man's companion, friend and muse. At last the cat knew deliverance.

It would serve no purpose to cite more texts or speak further of the past, or of the many famous men who have celebrated the cat. The last famous cat to be embalmed and mummified was that of Petrarch in about 1370. But there have been so many other distinguished cat-lovers; from Richelieu to Poincaré, from Disraeli to Taine, from Baudelaire to Mallarmé, from d'Aurévilly to Colette. 'Could there be' – Professor Henri Mondor has written – 'a kind of intimate, subtle aesthetic, a natural affinity between all those who have fallen under the cat's spell?'

What more touching homage could be paid to a creature

which, of all, is most fit to live free on earth, where his very arrival is a mystery, and where – indifferent to all the conflicting passions which his presence has inspired – the cat, enigmatic, grand and supreme, has phantom-like only passed.

II

What is He?

Deferential as one is, before expert psychology controlled by experiment, and as much as one approves of animal research free of anthropomorphism, one must admit the following: in an attempt to understand the cat, the analogical method cannot be rejected out of hand.

If concepts like Memory or Suffering have a common meaning for all the higher forms of life, and if one considers such words as Fidelity, Attachment, Curiosity as equally applicable to animals and man, it is necessary to apply and interpret them in delving into the psychological mysteries of the cat world.

But can one generalize? As if the 'cat world' were made up only of males! (Then, too, toms must be distinguished from neutered males.) The queens have their own individual ways; and here again divisions must be made between virgins, those who are mothers, and the neutered females. Finally there are kittens.

There are as many differences of behaviour among cats as there are between a man and a woman, or between the adult couple and their child.

Then one tends to imagine that that is the entire story, and so one hastens wrongly to declare that male cats are thieving, lazy and selfish, that queens are shameless and libidinous, that kittens are innocent and ingenuous.

It is not so simple. We shall try, however, through observation and science, to find out as exactly as possible – what the cat is.

2. THE CAT WORLD

Let us begin with some feline sociology: has the 'cat world' a community spirit like that of so many other animals: horses, elephants, wolves, monkeys or seals? Is the cat, for all his reputation as an egoist and sybarite, a social animal and capable of adapting to a communal existence?

A cat-fancier who, in less than ten years, has taken in over a thousand cats and reared over five hundred, all of whom were mangy, harassed and miserable to begin with, is categoric on this point:

'Put twenty dogs,' says Mme Jacques Rigoir, 'twenty dogs taken at random, under one common protecting roof, and they will fight all day – more or less histrionically, of course; but they will fight over a yes or no, an imagined look of defiance, or some stupid question of precedence.

'Sixty or eighty cats, on the other hand, will live in peace in a very restricted space; and, if the males are neutered, never a quarrel will disturb their tranquillity. What is more, they will sleep, most of them, massed in indistinguishable clusters, huddled warmly against each other. And if one who is on his own should suddenly feel chilly and want to burrow into the mass, he will approach gently, brushing himself against them, distributing licks and caresses as a kind of entrance-fee, and presently joining the crowd.

'Introduce a stranger, an unknown cat, into the place. He is the only one to get excited, to tremble at the idea of putting a foot wrong with the others. The old-stagers, apparently indifferent, blink, incline their chins almost imperceptibly, put their heads on one side and look at him, and finish, nine times out of ten, by adopting him.'

Here, of course, it is a question of cats without masters, of cats whose world is restricted to the communal room or wire enclosure reserved for them.

But what of the ones who are really on their own? Those who, having not even this shelter, go hungry, are at liberty to suffer and to make love, the 'strays'? Well, even these enjoy their meetings in some deserted yard, behind a hoarding or on top of a wall, where they put their heads together, exchange messages of comfort, troubles and fears, as well as desires.

MEMORY

There are, however, independent types, individualists to the bitter end. These are, in general, not the ones who have had a *master*, but those who have had a *friend*, those whom some human being has loved and petted and who, divorced from their environment, remember it and cannot live elsewhere.

Blondinette belonged in this category: and the story of that big black cat abandoned by her masters, for reasons that constitute no excuse, is rather strange.

After seven years! After seven years of warmth and purring, of an uninterrupted rhythm of regular meals and quiet naps. Seven years of that measured sameness of existence that neutered cats in particular find so congenial.

Her masters having left her, Blondinette was taken in by a friend who lavished affection on her in vain. Without being hostile or timid, Blondinette accepted her fate. She passed entire days on an armchair or some piece of furniture, indifferent to everything and everyone. A week, three weeks, passed. Blondinette neither ate nor drank. She was waiting –

not for death, which was an abstract idea quite beyond her scope – but for the improbable miracle which would give her back her home and the people she loved.

A month passed. For a whole month she had kept up this terrible reserve; and the friend, concerned, wrote to her former masters: 'If you have any pity, come and take back this creature, who is more faithful to the past than you have been. She is wasting away, eating nothing, dying with astonishing dignity.'

And the mistress wrote in answer a few lines of vague considerations and regrets, promising to send some short-bread biscuits which Blondinette used to like.

What unknown sense told the cat? The messenger had scarcely crossed the threshold when Blondinette with one bound jumped to the floor, ran towards him and miaowed, her tail erect and stiff as a taper: she was claiming 'her' short-bread. She ate one, two of them, drank a little of the milk that she had disdained to touch for several weeks; and the miracle was accomplished.

She had come out of her trance. The motor had begun to work again. In a few minutes she was the purring Blondinette of old. The unhappy cat was saved – saved by the prosaic memory of the senses, when the fatal poetry of remembering had been killing her insidiously.

What saved her was her olfactory memory to begin with, then memory through taste. But need we classify different kinds of memory as more or less worthy?

The astonishing thing with cats is just this ability to fasten on everything, to register and retain everything. Because, with his heritage of uneasiness and defensiveness, the cat, listening and observing all day, has far more memory than one would credit.

Miquet, a mangy, old, dirty-white tom, prowled about the port of Cannes where he had been hanging out for months. A compassionate woman happened by, took him up and carried him home, where she looked after him for three days, no longer. The first time the door was left open, Miquet, by now gorged and covered with pomade, gave her the slip.

A year passed. No Miquet; not a trace of him. Then one evening, thirteen months later, quite by chance Miquet and his woman-friend found themselves face to face.

'Why it's Miquet!' said the woman simply, much more surprised than the cat.

And the latter; the independent, unapproachable Miquet, went up to her and rubbed himself against her, purring and putting himself out to be friendly. Just like that, he recognized her. The woman, moved by this demonstration from a cat whom she knew to be unsociable, made as if to grab him and carry him away as before. With a squirming leap, he got out of her arms and in one jump was on the edge of a boat moored to the bank. From here, round-eyed, he stared at her like a grateful but ruffled tramp.

It is already something for a cat to remember someone who looked after him for a few hours. But why was the memory, by rights not very agreeable, in the long run mingled with sympathy and evident confidence, and without rancour or regret?

If the affective memory preponderates thus over the sensual memory, as is very often the case with cats, it is probably because they feel first and think afterwards, and then they judge and make allowance for things as we do – perhaps better than we do.

JEALOUSY

I call to mind Pussy-Kiki, Kiki-the-Tough, one of my cats who out of jealousy chose freedom one day and who, as his mood varied, was animated either by a desire for revenge or a covert affectionateness.

Son of an unknown father and a Spanish mother, he showed no trace of the tri-coloured maternal heritage. He was vaguely a dingy brown, ringed when the sun shone with unsuspected black circles.

Kipling affirmed that Shera the Tiger had acquired his striped coat when the jungle thickets, to punish him for his pride, whipped him as he passed. Pussy-Kiki, in the shadows of his foetal life, must have shown a similarly natural taste for squabbles, to be thus decorated with blows.

He was the sole survivor of a large litter. As soon as he could open his eyes and make a reeling attack, he threw himself on Miche who, good dog that she was, let him dig his claws into her tough griffon fleece. When he went too far, she growled amicably and sent him rolling, with a blow from her paw, to the other end of the big divan. But Pussy, growing bigger and fatter month by month, became tougher; and there was a splendid cavalcade across the garden one morning when, on the back of the galloping dog, he pretended to make her his horse, showing off before the whole household.

From that day on he was impossible. He uprooted the succulent plants, overturned vases of flowers on the piano, ripped open armchairs and inundated the legs of tables. In the interests of peace, we had him neutered; but this made not the slightest difference in the world to his character.

Bored at home, he set out on adventures of discovery, climbing the neighbours' gates and garden walls, and having rendezvous with all the stray cats of the area. Thus it came about that he felt insulted on the sensitive point of his manhood.

But the swaggering toms he met did not know the stuff of which he was made. Pussy, stout, strong, muscled like a panther, challenged them all to have it out. So the February nights were filled with unrelenting struggles, Homeric battles punctuated by the howling of provocations, the spitting that denoted fear, and an angry hissing.

When spring began to touch the edge of the privet copses with green, Pussy had leisure to polish his coat and lick his wounds. All the others had disappeared; he was alone. He slept on the roofs. He appeared in the dining-room first every other day, then once a week. As his mistress loved cats possessively and not to see them get away at the first opportunity or hear them being butchered all night, she adopted a little homeless cat, as white and sweet, as thin and timid as Pussy was a dour rebel, strapping and insolent.

From the next day, Pussy disappeared. For months there

was no news of him. Then one morning he appeared, strangely covered in pink wool and scented with patchouli. A discreet inquiry and some gossip revealed that he had become the darling of a certain neighbourhood house, discreetest of its kind, where he was known by the name of 'Kiki'.

Pussy-Kiki was sick now and had returned to the fold. But not for long. The prodigal son, lying there in a bad way, his eyes half-closed, his nose stopped up, remembered his childhood. He suffered all the medical rigours without a murmur. His ears flat against his skull, he let himself be daubed with revulsives and stabbed with burning needles. He suffered the vile inhalation and everything else, confined as he was to a basket placed on a cane-bottomed chair and covered with his master's dressing-gown.

He resigned himself for three days to undergoing all this treatment, by the end of which time he was breathing more easily. What was more, he had made up his mind about the new cat, that usurper and intruder whom he had lain in wait for so often in vain on the next-door wall, that intruder whom he had never seen for a single minute, either in the garden or on the window-sill.

She was here now. Only the thickness of the basket separated them. She was here, looking calm and proud and so sure of herself that it made him sick, with her enormous, ridiculous stomach made of god-knows-what, and that hypocrite's air she put on so sweetly of being interested in his health.

Kiki-the-Tough was not afraid of toms, but queens upset him. They humiliated him, without his knowing exactly why; so he hated the sight of them.

Now he kept quiet. Across the bars of his wicker prison, he saw her walk back and forth, sniffing mistrustfully, over the furniture. Then he heard her jog along suddenly to the kitchen with a little cry of joy. He recognized the familiar sound of 'his' bowl, that bowl in which he had drunk his first sips of milk, bit into his first pieces of raw heart, devoured his first leeks and discovered fresh cream; that bowl which he used to like upsetting with a single nudge when someone dared to serve him with cold noodles or suspect fish.

Kiki forgot his fever and his fiery throat of the previous

evening. Besides, he no longer felt that irritating ball that he had tried to cough up or to tear at from outside with his claws, that thing called angina.

In the evening he felt much better. He no longer needed 'them', nor anyone. They found out he was well again as soon as he was free to leap on to the table, jump to the top of the cupboard and come down a little later to slide under the chest in the corridor. They searched for him everywhere except in this dark hiding-place.

He was waiting for night and silence. When the time came, he sniffed the air, the hairs of his whiskers and eyebrows standing on end, risked a glance, and then, completely re-assured, made a dash for the kitchen. One leap up to the door-handle, which knew him of old and yielded to him. With a swipe of his paw, he opened the sideboard, gorged himself on mutton, made himself sick on cooking fat.

Suddenly from the floor below he heard the dog Miche, his old friend, who was uneasy. She was huffing discreetly at floor level near the door of 'their' room. He knew she would not bark, because she had recognized him, and, unless frightened or startled, dogs are generally considerate of their masters' sleep. But he understood that it would be dangerous to stay longer. Miche merely gave a low growl, a suitable greeting for an accomplice, when Kiki crossed the landing to reach the ground floor and from there the little basement door left open at night by the caretakers, which led to the service staircase and garage skylight.

The fresh air of the garden sobered him. The street was noiseless and deserted. Far away a stupid dog cried like a child. Then Kiki, avenged and satiated, yawned, stretched, licked his chest three times over, and let himself fall at the same time on to the gravel, where he slept, breathing in the noisome odours of 'his' dustbin, until the first hours of dawn.

We were not to see him again at the house for six months.

Jealous of his independence, and at the same time hurt by the idea that another could replace him so completely in his masters' affection, Pussy had returned to that other house where all strangers were welcome and where, without losing face or being far from us, he could be 'Kiki' while at the same time remaining the 'Pussy' of his young years.

The theory widely current today of a so-called 'territory'– that sense of a home ground which every animal knows perfectly and feels to be safe – is enough to explain why Pussy did not leave the neighbourhood; but are cats, as is commonly imagined, more attached to this home which is part of the 'territory' than to the people who live there? We shall see.

A week later war broke out. I had to leave almost immediately. My family also left the capital.

We returned to Paris only long after the armistice, in December. The next-door house was shut up, as was the elegant little mansion where Pussy used to play so happily in the midst of perfumed ladies. And we wondered, thinking of the frightful bombardments, the poverty and the winter cold, what had become of poor Kiki.

It was he who welcomed us. He was terribly thin, his fur pressed against his bones; and he limped (an accident or a fight?). But recognizing the sound of 'his' car, he had come up, crazy with delight, out of nowhere. His back arched and his tail a question-mark, he rubbed himself against 'his' door, against our suitcases, miaowing his desperate concern and joy.

How had he lived through such misery? Where had he found refuge against fear, hunger and cold? And what presentiment or sign had told him that we were coming back? Miche, the dog, was dead; and dead, too, the white cat, having littered in the midst of an air-raid. He knew that he was the survivor and for the future the only one, that he was once again the favourite.

As soon as the door was opened, he burst in, inspected every corner, sniffed each piece of furniture, worked himself into such a state that he could hardly breathe, and, as soon as it was dark, installed himself as by right on our bed, to sleep there for twenty-four hours.

Kiki-the-Tough proved more faithful than many human friends. He is dead now of old age, without having once, since that memorable return, gone beyond the garden door.

People who don't like cats (which is not a criticism) will continue to maintain that the cat is an indifferent creature, incapable of attachment, and that the apparent tenderness of so many Kikis springs in reality from the difficulties that cats, more than other animals, experience because they are too cowardly to venture far afield. Cats, they affirm, have a short memory; and ingratitude is second nature to them. To these self-appointed accusers, I dedicate this very authentic proof of their mistake:

About four years ago there died in mid-September at Pordic (Côtes-du-Nord) a kind old lady whose sole companion had been a large and amiable cat. They had a perfect understanding between them, and were always together day and night. He slept on her bed and shared her board. He followed her with his little steps in the garden, as patient, as discreet as a faithful dog.

The old lady's body was taken away. Friends, touched by the cat's devotion, adopted him. Since then he has lived very comfortably with them, four miles at least from the house where he had been happy with his beloved mistress for six years.

Now every year, when mid-September comes, this animal, so often described as egoistic, leaves his new masters and goes away – on a pilgrimage. He goes to the deserted villa where, three or four times a year, a charwoman comes to open the shutters and air the house. He is scarcely over the gate when he miaows his impatience. If the woman has not yet arrived, he stalks back and forth on the steps, then keeps circling the house. When she comes, she has hardly half-opened the door when he bounds in, crosses the passage, climbs to the first floor, inspects the empty room corner by corner, then descends again, sniffs the furniture, goes out, smells a flower near the gate, and goes slowly home.

How long does this visit last? Scarcely an hour. The cat then returns to his present master (who knows all about this annual pilgrimage), jumps on to an armchair and falls asleep or broods. And so it goes on until, the next year, always on that anniversary of September, some unknown force will come to remind him, in this extraordinary way, that it is time to remember.

Fiction? No, in this case there are definite facts, attested witnesses; and if you hesitate to admit that cats can 'conjure up', be faithful to the past, and have 'emotional memory', you must at least admit that in certain conditions of time, environment and climate they can rediscover, as we can, emotions long buried, thus clinging to the beloved past.

'Three or four miles? Yes, perhaps that's possible after all,' it has been said to me: 'but beyond that your cat would have stayed quietly at home, incapable of going very far without running great risks.'

But there are many cases of cats finding their way home through the utmost danger and the most bewildering conditions. There is the story of Blacky, a black cat belonging to M. Dutilleul, postmaster at Gironcourt-sur-Vraine, in the Vosges.

His master, who was moving house, set out one morning with all his possessions in a wagon. Blacky, who was getting on in years, was also making the move, shut up in a box. But as they rode along, his master changed his mind about the cat. After nearly three hours, M. Dutilleul un-nailed the box, let the cat out into the country, and continued on his way. At the village there was some comment about this surprising decision but soon it was forgotten.

Then one evening, a month later, the clerks at the Giron-court post office heard a cat scratching at the door. They opened; it was Blacky, unrecognizable and starving. He crept towards his favourite place, his master's office, and collapsed. They offered him milk and a bit of minced meat; he tasted it out of pure politeness. Next day he died, after having survived the gruelling adventure of living by hunting or theft, avoiding cars, animals and people; and walking, walking for hours and days, weeks and weeks, overcoming a hundred obstacles just in order to find that master whom, unhappily, he worshipped.

SENSE OF ORIENTATION

There are hundreds of such stories of cats finding their way home. They imply a courage and physical endurance transcending every privation: qualities which cats are rarely conceded to have.

Most people raise the same question. How can a cat, knowing nothing of a particular road or countryside, retrace his route along it? They speak of a sixth sense. But the cat has no sixth sense, in the accepted meaning of the term.

Méry, a Provencal ancester of mine, wrote the following account in one of his books about animals:

'In 1842 there lived a very old and melancholy cat belonging to the keeper of the Marseilles Museum. This ailing creature had lost all the characteristics of his kind: he no longer groomed himself with his paw, or sat in the sphinx position, or took any interest in the witches' sabbath, or sat at a window watching the dogs pass; everything was a matter of indifference to him.

'At Memphis four thousand years ago he would have been looked after; but in our age cats are accused of working evil in return for evil, and dogs are the preferred animals. Cats are victims of their own reasoning power and justice. When they are no longer young, they are not even regarded as cats any more, but are looked on askance, heaped with insults, and only seek some dark corner in which to drag out the last days of their old age. Then one can read in their eyes and the wrinkles on their foreheads what they think of man's ingratitude and the capriciousness of children.

'As the result of a conspiracy at the Museum, it was decided that this cat, whose only crime was old age, should be put in a sack and given to a keeper to be thrown from the summit of the Saut du Maroc into the sea. The Saut du Maroc is a sharp crag on the road to Rove, seven miles from Marseilles.

'The brute carried out these instructions without a qualm.

The cat, regaining all the strength of his youth at his final hour, struggled, using what remained of his teeth and claws; but the man had a hide like leather and would not let go. He pulled the cat out of the sack and swung him into the abyss.

'This cruel act had been devised in a Museum filled with Egyptian relics and mummies of cats dating from the time of the Pharaohs.

'Fourteen months later, the Keeper of the Museum, returning at midnight, heard a sharp, intermittent cry. As he looked, just for the record, at the embrasure of an inner window, he saw the old cat of the Saut du Maroc in the posture of a supplicant. Next day, in the sun, at an hour when ghosts can no longer walk, he saw the cat again, this time nonchalantly sitting on a mat in front of the Museum door. At once there was a great general reaction in favour of this indomitable creature, who from then on was overwhelmed with kindness and affection. His future provided for, he grew young again, returning gradually to the pursuits of his youth.

'Cats who are treated as beasts are aware of comparative misery and happiness, and adopt an attitude consistent with their lot. The unhappy cat abandons all his interests, becomes resigned and careless, and takes on the air of a Stoic philosopher conducting a perpetual monologue on life's vicissitudes. But at the least indication of hope, he sheds his indolence, pricks up his ears, goes out into the sun, parades haughtily in public, and refurbishes himself in his own eyes by combing and cleaning his fur. It was thus with the cat of the Saut du Maroc. No one recognized him any more.

'At this time I had quarters in the Museum of Marseilles [Méry continues], and I made every effort to work out the details of the cat's return. I discussed the question with the Director of the Natural History Museum, and we even made a day's pilgrimage together to the Saut du Maroc. From up there, looking down on a distant Marseilles surrounded by hills, villas and the sea, we understood less than ever how the cat could possibly have found his way home again.

'But I canvassed the problem unremittingly, and one day a chance succession of thoughts put the answer into my head.

'The hearing of cats, like that of birds, is so extremely delicate that the human ear is a deaf thing by comparison.

'Now the cat from the Museum, ineffectively thrown from the Saut du Maroc, had probably clung to the pines and saxifrages covering the mountain. Recovered from his fright, and like all his kind tenacious of life, he must have thought intently about how to regain his childhood home, from which he had been snatched by some unknown person.

'The cat had never seen the sea, that immense monster raging below. Instinctively, then, the unhappy creature avoided it. Having reached the quiet summit of a hill, he listened and heard in the dawn a far-away noise that he recognized: the sound of a great city wakening, the chiming of clocks, rolling of barrels and the clatter of wheels. ''The city is there, over there'', he said to himself, and set off towards it.

'A travelling cat is not without resources in the country. He can live by hunting: there is an abundance of game, from grasshoppers and cicadas to field-rats and frogs. These are a help; but there are also inconveniences. There are the hunters from Marseilles who, after an unsuccessful day, will revenge themselves on the first cat they meet. There are the peasants, jealous of their warrens; and the dogs who take it on themselves to bark at all the coaches and horses passing on the great road and incidentally making it dangerous. An old cat of experience can scent these dangers from a distance and avoid them. Finally, the cat is endowed with marvellous patience. He knows how to lie low all day in a safe place and wait for the dark night, time of prudence, when his phosphorescent eye can guide him along the unknown and hostile route.

'Our traveller was able to get across the country without accident, always guided by the city's noises which grew more distinct each day. It was already an achievement to have reached the city toll-houses; but now he had to find one house in a city of 160,000 souls, a city which he had crossed once only – and in a sack.

'In Marseilles, as in Constantinople, every sailor owns a dog to which he is devoted, but which at the moment of sailing he abandons in some inn. The dog, deprived of his master, will spend his life in searching through all the quarters of Marseilles. In Constantinople it has been like this since Mahomet II.

'Our cat was well aware of this danger. For ten years, from the vantage point of a Museum window, he had seen every canine type, from the enormous Mastiff to the King Charles Spaniel, file by. He would have to go carefully and feel his way, avoiding daylight and trusting only to darkness. He would have to reconnoitre from spyholes in cellars, live frugally, be content with little, like the rat in Horace, and move on every day before dawn in order to get nearer to his house and gain ground towards his goal.

'A great hubbub, mingling all the sounds and clamours, had told him the point on the horizon where the city lay. Once arrived in Marseilles he counted on a particular and familiar sound which would indicate the quarter where he had been born. So long as he did not hear this special sound, he had to walk, continue to walk, avoiding men, children and the daylight.

'Now the City Museum has a clock which is always sounding: not only the hours, but the quarters and the eighths; and it prefaces each sounding by a light cavatina by way of prelude. For ten years the cat had heard this loquacious clock overhead; in his youth he had often played with its pendulums. So long as, wandering from cellar to cellar, he did not hear this well-known chime, he told himself, "I am not on the right track. It must be farther."

'Without impatience or discouragement, he continued on taking the same precautions, listening to the clocks and never hearing his, the one he would have recognized in a concert of all the clocks of Italy.

'Chance, which never favours the unfortunate, might have led him sooner in the right direction and spared him much anguish; but, taking into account the length of his absence, fourteen months, one can only suppose that he came the longest way round, and reached the Museum quarter only after traversing all the crossroads of the old city.

'If only he could have written this odyssey; it would be difficult to imagine anything more moving. The number of dangers that he braved, the calculations he had to make, must have been prodigious. And when finally he heard in the distance, at midnight, the prolonged chiming of the clock, he had not yet finished: he had still some way to go and many battles to wage.

'To begin with, he could not let himself be carried away heedlessly by his joy. So near his goal, he must not compromise his chances of success by being hasty. A human being at a similar moment would have failed, but the animal manoeuvred as cautiously as on his first day. He mastered that treacherous joy that might have blinded him to possible dangers. He left nothing to chance, up to the last gutter, the last wall, the last step. And he arrived safe and sound.

'What a lesson for man, who arrives at absurdities by reflecting, who learns mathematics and then argues that two and two make five, who studies maps only to be smashed on reefs.'

THERE IS NO SIXTH SENSE

This is rather a lesson for the modern experts who tend to be a bit scornful of literary men like my ancestor Méry. Despite all the experimental tests, the laboratory mazes, conditioned reflexes and all the daily progress made by that new science called physio-psychology, no one, before Méry, had offered a valid solution to this problem. The fact of giving it a name, 'the sense of orientation', has not really answered this obscure question of animal behaviour, a question which is still being gone into.

True, my ancestor overlooked the fact that the cat is not only an auditive creature, but that his eyes, his whiskers and eyebrows are excellent antennae. And he disregarded the cat's sense of smell and marvellous sensitivity of touch; but all the same Méry showed the way. Today, of course, we know that dogs and cats can find their way by a series of stages combining the auditory, visual, olfactive and kinaesthetics.

But as yet we hardly know how to use this information: the animal mechanism has not yet revealed all its secrets. A man knows how to travel, starting with an abstract idea of where he wants to go, and then planning his itinerary. But how does the cat reflect? And does it or does it not reflect before launching out on an adventure?

We must not make the mistake of imagining that animals are the more reflective because they appear to act so slowly, as if taking a decision before each step. The time they take has nothing to do with the case. One dog, put on a fresh scent, will set off at a gallop and reach his goal in ten minutes; another, launched on the same track, will take two days, losing and recovering the thread.

So cats seem to advance at random, led astray as they are twenty times for every useful perception that starts a familiar association for them. They will think: 'This stony road, and this dog who barks on two notes? It is the big farm where the milk flows like water.' And it is probably the same with odours recognized from familiar sounds or things seen, from which a link is more or less quickly forged, leading them on to attain, by their tentative fumblings and efforts, what we would call the goal, but what to them is the purely unconscious ending of their hazardous exploits.

BEYOND THE PALE OF SCIENCE

'But then, all the rest is literature?' you may ask.

Certainly not.

Even in those of her writings where Colette, for example, has taken most liberties with scientific fact, there is always a thread of plausibility. There is that passage where the reader is made to imagine himself as a cat. I should like to quote those lines on 'Kiki-the-Sweetie', where the reader cannot help 'thinking as a cat', so sure is the observation.

'If I wished,' said Kiki-the-Sweetie, 'I could easily curl up in a chair that was badly wedged, and its legs would hammer in rhythm – tic-toc, tic-toc, tic-toc – to the rhythm of my tongue. This is my trick when I want to get out. Tic-toc, tic-toc, tic-toc, the chair says. She, as she is reading, gets annoyed and cries, "Quiet Kiki!" Standing on my rights, I continue to wash, all innocence. Tic-toc, tic-toc, tic-toc. She jumps up in a fury, and throws the door wide open for me. Walking like an exile, I hesitate, before going through.

'Once outside, I laugh, laugh, to feel myself above everything.'

Doubtless this attributing of machiavellianism to cats is rather guesswork; but why after all should cats not be capable, like men, of quite simply associating the wished-for results of an opening door with the noise of a rickety chair? Why should we doubt that a cat, having seen a second phenomenon automatically follow from a first on several occasions, would be capable of provoking the first in order that the second (more complicated and not dependent on him) might happen?

What is perhaps pure literature, in this excerpt from Colette, is the idea that a cat can know that a certain noise will displease her mistress. And yet, will we ever know what cats are thinking about?

Mischievous, artful, restless, they sometimes display rather disconcerting qualities. Queens especially become jealous, often for odd reasons: like those two little Siameses, mother and daughter, who shared a mate in common and three times a year were obliged by him impartially. But this was not the reason for their private quarrel.

Chance would have it that each time their kittens were born almost simultaneously. The mother would have five or six, the daughter two or three, no more. They never fought. They were perfectly tranquil about the shared mate. But from the first hours of life of their respective offspring, everything changed. They watched each other covertly; and every day the daughter, taking advantage of a temporary absence of her mother, would pilfer, according to the situation, two or three kittens, with as much address as numerical exactness. Why? Probably out of jealousy: but clearly all she wanted was to have the same number of kittens as her mother (who, by the way, always recovered them straight away and popped them back into her own basket).

As for toms, they are equally complicated. Doudou, an old queen taken in from the streets one January evening, was as clean as any other cat; but Philibert only half tolerated her. For a long time we considered her the most modest cat we had ever known! At nightfall she would creep under a piece of furniture and quite readily let herself be shut up in some room or other. Then, in the silence of the house when everyone was asleep, she would relieve herself at last. In the morning we would discover the substance of the offence in a corner of the sitting-room or under a seat.

Despairing of training her, we were thinking seriously of sending her to the country when a more perceptive friend who was spending a few days with us discovered the truth and the injustice of the case. Philibert (who is male only in name) was behaving with the most disgusting selfishness towards Doudou. Not only did he insist that she should eat only after him, but he hounded her from every corner, from the tiles by the radiator, from the seats of armchairs, from the tops of cupboards; and as they shared a sanitary tray, each time he surprised her there, he leaped on her and drove her away at once.

It was left for poor Doudou to relieve herself in secrecy, where she could hope to have a little peace, and preferably at night.

CURIOSITY

Cats are more curious than the most inquisitive women: curious about the contents of a parcel one is carrying, curious about every new object, which they will sniff round completely before reassuring themselves, with a discreet touch of the paw, that 'the thing' is inanimate. Curious about the visitor, whom they will either watch from a distance or approach closely, according to whether he appears hostile or sympathetic. Curious about the comings and goings of people passing in the street. More curious than one could possibly imagine, even about the lives of their masters.

I know one who pushes her curiosity well beyond her own home-ground. This is Mitzi, the blue-grey cat belonging to a village priest some miles from Orléans. Mitzi follows his master everywhere. On a mild summer night, should the priest be walking to the nearby town to visit a colleague, the cat follows at his heels. Two and a half miles there, and three and a half back again (they return by the banks of the Loire): but it would take more than this to discourage Mitzi, who comes out simply to know where his master is going.

Perhaps also, you may think, for the pleasure of having a moonlight sniff and hunt round the fields? Not a bit of it. Mitzi is above all curious. He is equally willing to play the chaperon and accompany the ladies of the parish. There is not a charity evening, not a sale or a ball at which he does not appear, creeping in behind some acquaintance and opening his great golden eyes on everyone who comes and goes or moves about in the light and noise. He stays there an hour or two, then returns discreetly to the presbytery. And throughout the day he spends entire hours looking through the window.

No one knows if he is a thief or a gourmand: he is curious.

DEXTERITY

Dexterous? No one can doubt it who has ever watched these born acrobats with their sense of distance and the fragility of objects – just as seals have a sense of balance, sleepwalkers immunity from giddiness, and bats the power of avoiding obstacles in the dark.

I am always surprised, when I visit a collector friend of mine, to see two big cats moving about in the midst of his porcelain or sleeping between two crystal Buddhas. The master of the house does not turn a hair. 'I have always had cats, big and small,' he declares. 'In twenty years they have never knocked against the least trinket. However! One day one of them as he stretched out toppled a vase over – the only one which had no commercial value: it was imitation.'

Dexterous at managing such things, at opening doors, at getting a cake out of the fire without burning themselves. Skilful to the point of invention, of adapting themselves to circumstances, like Dr Lafourcade's cat, which had a passion for sparrows.

He hunted them from cover. Patiently, without moving a

hair, he would watch for the favourable moment to leap, to the great despair of his master. 'How,' the Doctor asked himself, 'am I to satisfy my shameful weakness for spoiling this monster without being a party to the murder of these poor birds?'

And the idea came to him to attach a bell to the cat's collar.

The birds caught on quite quickly. So long as the cat, still as a statue, did not make the least movement, there was no danger for them. But at the slightest impulse of attack, the bell tinkled and, warned in time, the sparrows flew away.

Frustrated, the cat pondered. After several days of failure, he ended by realizing that this wretched bell was working against him.

Chance – or was it something else? – made him notice another thing: when he charged with his head down, the bell did not sound.

This was enough. Two days later he was found smacking his lips, some feathers scattered around him. Observing him, the Doctor discovered the method of his cunning: he would wait, flattened on the ground, his tail softly beating the air with greed and impatience, and then would make one single bound on his unsuspecting prey, his chin held down against his neck to prevent the bell from doing its office.

'And since then,' the Doctor told me, with a sad but secretly admiring expression, 'when we hear the bell make a brief sound, first cautious, then suddenly definite, we know that that tinkling means a new victory for our crafty rascal.'

CRAFT

His craft the cat shows at every turn; and those who, out of scientific curiosity – like Professor Binet, dean of the Faculty of Medicine in Paris – have studied him quite impartially, have had to agree with this.

'A vacuum having been created one day in a bell-glass where a cat had been placed,' wrote Professor Binet, 'the animal collapsed very quickly, only to recover automatically as soon as air was reintroduced into the vacuum.

'The next day he could not be caught unawares. As soon as the suction pump was put into operation, the cat was observed to put his paw gently on the opening through which the air was pumped out; then he withdrew it when he saw that the air was being let in again.

'Thereafter we recorded the same reaction in every experiment. It had taken this little cat less than an hour to understand!'

ADDRESS

Similarly, if his address, the sureness of his reflexes, are compared with those of other animals, which of them could equal him?

A puppy of several months old is clumsiness itself compared with a cat scarcely three weeks old who is making a bit of paper turn in the air. Watch him imitate the hunt, all the secrets of which he knows already. Young as he is, he knows all the phases; the delighted quivering in the place of cover, the snake-like advance, the gentle swaying motion of the hindquarters controlling the exact power of the leap, and then the lightning flash of the attack, in which every muscle and gesture has a predetermined role.

The kitten's adroitness grow with him. At two months he can leap like a ballerina, to seize the curtain cords or reach the rabbit's foot hung at the end of a string from the door-knob. Mousing is really too simple now. He practises jumping, to be able to catch birds in flight. He lifts latches, opens doors.

And then there are cats who fish. Nothing is guesswork to them: neither the swiftness of the fish, nor the strength of the current, nor the refraction of light by the water.

Anxious to be further informed on the adroitness of certain animals, the experts, who accept no information second-hand, wished to establish the conditions in which animals make use of their extremities. They tested monkeys, rabbits, squirrels, rats and parrots for this, and ended up with cats. Professor J. Cole of Oxford published the results of this research.

Man, of course, shows a marked preference for using the right hand. But the cat – is he the more adroit with one member than the other? Now, contrary to the above mentioned animals, the cat does not generally feed himself with his paws. It was necessary, then, for the purpose of this experiment, to force him to do so.

Sixty cats, taken at random, all adult and of different kinds and sexes, were the subject of the test: twenty-seven were male and thirty-three female. The apparatus? A tube of solid glass about six inches long and three in diameter, attached to a block of wood, and so removable for disinfecting and cleaning. The cats had to thrust a paw into this tube in order to get hold of a titbit which they find irresistible: raw rabbit.

As soon as the animals had been made familiar with this new receptacle, the experiment began. Every day it was noted carefully how often each cat used one paw or the other. The standard adopted to estimate preference was that used by Professors Tsaï and Maurer in their study of rats: if a cat reached for the titbit with a particular paw at least 75 per cent of the time, he was considered as showing a preference for that paw.

(The strictest opponents of animal experimentation can be easy here. This experiment, harmless as it was, delighted the participants, who dashed up miaowing with impatience to take part.) Let us summarize the results.

The same studies previously made by Tsaï and Maurer on rats had shown rats to be predominantly right-handed, while the majority of parrots proved left-handed (Friedman and Davis); monkeys showed an equal proportion of right-handed and left-handed ones, with a very few ambidextrous (Finch and Yerkes).

And cats? The experiment showed their adroitness: an adroitness all the more marked as, unlike birds, rats and monkeys, cats are not accustomed to using their paws to eat.

The cats in Professor Cole's experiment responded in a surprising fashion: half of them used the right or left paw with an equal frequency. So more than half were ambidextrous, as of the thirty cats remaining, twelve had to be eliminated because of their frivolous behaviour. As for the eighteen who seemed to prefer one paw to the other, almost all were left-handed.

So then, cats are far more adroit with their extremities than are the majority of rats, parrots, monkeys and men. But of course we thought so all the time.

3. MYSTERIES AND MISUNDERSTANDINGS

It is true that the cat ought not to be used as a guinea-pig; that he ought, on the contrary, to be able to eat, drink, make love, muse and sleep as and when he likes. Men owe him that after having persecuted him throughout the centuries. But there are so many misunderstandings between him and them.

The first was the wish to domesticate an animal which is not domesticable to the point of strict dependence. And in thousands of years the cat has not changed: he is barely tame.

All other animals, by inclination or necessity, bend to us; but we bend to the cat, who obeys no one.

Have you ever tried to make a cat come indoors, when he has been lounging in the garden or sleeping on the roof in the sun all morning? He turns a deaf ear to all your calls and threats, and is merely amused by your flattery. But if it is he who decides to come in, he gives the order, and of course you finish by opening the door to him, that door of whose existence he had seemed so innocently unaware until then.

One can never bully a cat. You want to quieten him? He turns lively. You wish to corner him? He runs away. This characteristic gives rise to thousands of mistakes which informed as well as ignorant people make every day.

A similar one is the glorious excuse made by selfish or miserly people who don't feed their cat, because cats, they assert, eat rats. This is quite untrue: a cat will kill rats, but not eat them. It is true that people readily confuse mice and rats.

Therefore it is not such an optional matter for scientific accuracy to intervene in many cases either to quash mistakes or to confirm traditional truths.

THE CAT AND HIS DOMAIN

'What is the use of all this?' the ignorant will ask: 'It is exactly the same as with human beings, and everything leads us to believe ... '

Not a bit of it. All is not 'exactly the same as with human beings'. The truth is only the facts proven by the latest research of the Institute of Animal Psychology at Buldern in Westphalia, together with the fruits of our daily observation. Like birds, lions and most creatures who have their liberty, cats live in an exterior world very straitly determined, in a 'territory' established and ruled by very strict laws whose principles they obey.

This 'territory', this domain to which we have previously alluded, might be subdivided into two or three successive belts, the boundaries of which correspond to various fields of activity; from the epicentre, which can be both the place where the cat will litter and bring up its young and the preferred sleeping-place; to the hunting-ground zone; and between them an intermediate zone, the familiar zone. The cat would regard the latter as a safe playground, but would concede that his squatter's rights there are partially disputable.

In the first zone the cat is completely at home; and the tranquillity and affection which he feels there come from his masters' attachment to him. The walls of the apartment bound it. All the chairs, the corners and recesses, the closets, cupboards and furniture are part of it. One can never tell exactly why a cat stakes his claim on such or such a particular place in the house. Why, for example, of five armchairs exactly alike that furnish my office, does a certain one of my cats choose one to which he always goes, even if the cushion is changed or the positions altered?

The second zone begins where, beyond the threshold, the landing or the street begins. This is the zone of independence, which must be respected if the cat is not to feel his bondage. This zone is, generally, of about the same extent as the first.

For our big cat Philibert, crotchety, precise, an excellent example, that zone for a long time did not go beyond the first hundred square yards of the garden and the roof of the garage. It was there that, for almost a year, he played at being his own master, neglecting the beloved armchair to go sightseeing on the uncomfortable roof.

After this period, during which matters were being weighed and considered, came the call of adventure. He advanced to the third zone, which extended farther, for several hundred yards, including the neighbours' gardens.

This third zone is, for city cats where space is limited, the zone of uncertainty, of exploration, of uneasiness, temptation and audacity. For those living in blocks of flats, it is the zone of the flat upstairs (or more rarely downstairs). For cats that are free and sure of themselves it is the sector of mousing or bird-watching, where they take their chances and also assume certain rights and duties in regard to the other neighbourhood cats, and where they take care not to be caught napping. This is the region of expeditions and hunting.

To get from one of these zones to another, a cat will have established routes with personal landmarks, going by the sense of smell, and also with points of security which are positions of shelter and possible retreat prepared in advance.

It is the same kind of sensitivity that certain nervous women have who can only get across London by telling themselves: 'If I feel bad in Baker Street I can always drop in on the Joneses. The Smiths live in Hampstead, quite near too . . .'

The cat, for all his reputation of being independent and capricious, does not venture out carelessly. He moves through his territory with the regularity of a railway schedule. My friend Philibert will never go to the left of the last step of the staircase leading to the garden. Always at the same time, he runs along the wall to the right, in exactly the same place jumps to the garage roof, then goes to the middle gate, and after pausing briefly by the chestnut tree (to signal his crossing), goes to scratch at my neighbour's studio door.

What hidden clock warns him twice a day that it is meal-time; and what is it that tells him, on summer evenings, that it is time to go home, to creep under the iron curtain that will come down in two minutes?

What chronological-cum-musical sense enables him to dif-ferentiate at the same time (when he is sleeping in a garden at least fifty yards from the kitchen) between the sound of the crockery being got ready for the table and the jingle of that (similar in every way) which is kept for him?

Small mysteries which we shall try to solve by studying the psycho-physiology of the cat and by trying, as we go, to clear up some classic and unwarranted misunderstandings.

CAN THE CAT GET ON WITH THE DOG?

Among many other prejudices, the most widespread is that which considers the cat and the dog as enemies. And yet numerous examples reveal possibilities of understanding, complicity and perhaps true friendship between these two species.

There is that fierce Borzoi in whose sight no representative of the feline kind found favour, but who slept with his mess-mate, a baby Siamese, between his paws.

Some friends of ours had a blue-grey cat who, out of friend-ship for the old spaniel of the house, entered into rather a strange intrigue. The dog, having nearly died twice as a result of his unwise taste for fowl, was tied up in the garden to avoid an accident every time chicken or rabbit appeared on his masters' bill-of-fare. And then one day they discovered that the cat was stealing regularly. Profiting by a moment of in-attention on their part, he would get hold of a bone at the end of a course, run into the garden and lay it down in front of the dog's nose, and with obvious satisfaction watch his old friend's treat.

But the following is more touching still:

In a certain country farm, the cat had just given birth to five kittens in the hayloft. The farmer, discovering these future useless mouths to feed, drove the mother away brutally, seized her young without showing the least gentleness, and went to bury them in a corner of the garden. Alive! The five babies were alive, but barely a few hours old, deaf and blind (as they would have been for the next ten days), and so insensible of the horror.

When the man had finished, the cat, who was watching from a tree-top, came down, and quickly, quickly, started to scratch at the earth as best she could, pausing from time to time to make sure that the man was not coming back. But the claws of cats are scissors rather than picks, and the paws of the unhappy creature were soon bleeding, without her having been able to rescue her babies.

What voice then warned her that there was not a minute to lose? By what psychic path, by what train of psychosensory changes did the 'idea' come to her mind? She bolted towards the kennel, to the kitchen. She was looking for the dog! She found him asleep near the stable door.

One would like to hear a scientist's account of this, an account of the workings of the neurocentric machinery, explaining all that followed. The dog yawned, stretched and leapt to the cat's side. Very quickly she led him to the place.

The dog sniffed the ground, gave one or two tentative barks, then impatient little cries. He too began to scratch, to scratch at the ground. He dug frantically. The soil flew up under his paws. Once or twice he stopped to sniff down, thrusting his entire muzzle into the hole, which was yawning deeper second by second. And presently something appeared.

Without waiting, the cat jumped down to the bottom of this little grave. She fretted, even biting at the earth. She finished by unearthing the first kitten, which she carried away. The dog followed with the second.

Two minutes later she was once again in the hayloft.

The dog went back immediately. He returned with a third half-dead survivor, which he placed between its mother's paws – then a fourth, a fifth; and each time the cat ran to the trap-door, leaning down from the top of the ladder and welcoming the dog and his burden with purrs of joy.

Then she revived and restored her five kittens, soiled as they were with earth and saliva.

The farm shepherd, a boy of fifteen, amazed at the cat's manoeuvre, that evening told his mistress about the incredible rescue. The farmer, in his turn, was told, and took pity on the cat.

Since then the cat and her kittens have died of kindness and old age, and the young shepherd has grown up. He manages a farming estate near Vichy, and has three children now. It was he who told me the story, adding that no one but an utter brute, after witnessing this scene, could have failed to become an admirer and friend of cats.

THE CAT IS THE SLAVE OF HIS SYMPATHETIC NERVE

What other animal mother could have acted thus? No female but the cat has this speed of adaptability, or possesses to so high a degree those lightning reactions of alertness, those emergency reactions that American experts in particular have studied.

To what are they owing exactly? To the sympathetic nerve, the unsuspected possibilities in the sympathetic system of the cat for responding instantly to the most exacting needs.

A somewhat painful experiment has shown this. Doubtless its permissibility is disputable; but it revealed the abyss that, psychologically speaking, separates the dog from the cat.

Professor Cannon and his students have experimented by removing two sympathetic ganglionary chains from cats. A cat mutilated in this way, if kept in exceptional living conditions, well housed and fed, and protected against every change in temperature, will differ in no respect from a normal cat. He will simply have some difficulty in raising his third eyelid (that nictitating membrane covering the eye of most carnivores); but if after his recovery he is put among normal cats, without being given a special diet or protected against cold, it is evident that many of his functions are disturbed. He cannot leap about happily like the others, he refuses to fight back against the merest little kitten, and at the sight of a dog, instead of arching his back or running away, his fear nails him to the ground or makes him fall into a faint.

In the same conditions of experiment, what is the effect on a dog?

Russian, English and Japanese researchers have tried these procedures of Cannon's on the dog. Their findings were conclusive: a dog operated on in just the same conditions is completely the same without his sympathetic ganglionary chains. Following the operation, he will jump, fight, show anger or pleasure, without revealing inferiority or fatigue, and his thermeropletive functions are unchanged.

So then, the dog shows no effects when deprived of his sympathetic nerve, while the cat is a slave to it.

Here is where one's ordinary observations and those of science coincide.

'A scalded cat dreads cold water,' an old French proverb says. This is true, but only in a relative, not in an absolute, sense; for the cat doesn't fear water because it is cold. There are numerous cats who bathe and also go out in any weather.

Philibert-Pasha, for example, has never forgotten his year as a mascot of a steamer. He survived tornadoes on the Indian Ocean and typhoons on the China Sea. As a mere kitten of three months, he remained on the bridge when it was swept by waves, just for the sport of springing aside and being deliciously afraid, and for the pleasure of making his rounds of the kitchen afterwards and being regaled like a real sailor.

Turned landsman in Paris, he kept his old habits. He drinks from the taps of basins, and circles round the bath's shining rim; his cup is full when after a downpour he can splash in the puddles of water or the sodden grass of the garden.

No, the cat does not fear cold water because it is cold; and the saying 'A scalded cat . . . ' expresses simply and empirically the lightning reactions of an aggravated nervousness.

If one were to throw some boiling water at a cat, it would be enough to ensure that later the same gesture with cold water would cause an identical reflex action. The cat does not stop to reflect. He doesn't waste time, as the dog would, in trying to discriminate between possible consequences.

Equally classic is the common remark: 'Watch that cat . . . It is going to rain.'

Cats are uneasy some hours before a storm. They do not stop licking their fur, which the erectile muscles prick up at the least alarm. If the threat grows more definite, keep an eye on them; they keep wetting their paws and passing it behind their ear, that receiving station which, sensitive as it is, attracts so many unknown waves.

Science explains this phenomenon too; if the cat passes his paw over his ear, it is to try to calm himself, to mitigate the effect of the electric waves which keep going through him maddeningly when the storm is slow in starting. Then the first drops fall, and the cat, immediately relaxed, jumps on to his armchair, curls up and goes to sleep.

Cats are not often relaxed. Alertness and wariness is their way. They sleep with one eye half-open, and at the least need can react in the space of one-fiftieth of a second.

I had an experience of this one day, in the course of a curious incident.

I had been called in several times by a client who owned two cats which hated each other: a pure-bred Siamese and a so-called 'ordinary' striped cat. Their mutual hatred was so violent that they had to be watched very closely: 'Look out! Mitsou is there. Hold Miquette!' And the whole house had to play a careful game, for days on end, with barricaded doors and excessive precautions against the dreaded clash.

That morning I had come to treat the Siamese. When I rang the bell, they were just trying to get hold of the striped cat Miquette. They looked for her under all the furniture, but in vain.

I treated the Siamese, giving her an injection. Mitsou was quite used to it; but suddenly, as I drove in the needle, she cried out. And the scene immediately developed in the most lightning manner.

Miquette, the enemy, hurling herself down from the top of

an enormous wardrobe from which she had watched everything, had just leapt on my back and was tearing at my shoulders.

Don't imagine that she was coming to the aid of the sick cat. Far from it. Her attack over, it was on the invalid that she rushed to revenge herself for that stupid panic in which, because of an unaccustomed cry and in spite of all her hatred, she had obeyed by reflex action.

DOES THE CAT ALWAYS FALL ON HIS FEET?

'The cat,' it is said, 'always falls on his feet.' The Arabs would have it that he owes this privilege to Mahomet.

Is the saying true? Two hundred and fifty years ago the Academy of Science considered this problem in a somewhat fanciful way:

'When they jump from a high place, cats generally fall on their feet, even if they aim them upwards at that second and ought therefore to fall on their head! Fear, gripping them, makes them curve their spine, thus pushing the intestine forward [sic]. At the same time they stretch out their head and legs towards the place they have fallen from, as though to get back there: which gives those parts a great motive power. Thus their centre of gravity tends to be different from, or higher than, the centre of the body. From which it follows that these animals must make a half-turn in the air and fall on their paws, which saves their lives.'

I leave you to work it out!

In 1895, happily, Marey, having recourse to chronophotography, at the speed of sixty images per second, demonstrated (as today the slow-motion camera could do) that a cat thrown head-first into space makes a forward somersault of about 180°, and then an equal backward one. The hypothesis of a support by the resistance of the air is not permissible.

'By reason of the animal's sense of movement,' said Marey, 'if that resistance had really appreciable effects, an inverse rotation from that which is recorded would be produced.'

One may well wonder that the cat can turn in this way without any force or exterior support intervening. One admits certainly that a material body, yielding only to gravity and tending to repose, cannot impart to itself a rotation round a horizontal axis passing through its centre of gravity. But the fact is there, indisputable. And Professor Marey specified:

'It is in the inertia of its own mass that the animal finds the support enabling it to turn. The pair of twistings produced by the action of the vertebrate muscles acts first on the forequarters, which at the moment of inertia are very weak because the anterior members are at that moment clutched against the neck. The back ones, on the other hand, being stretched out and almost perpendicular to the body, give a moment of inertia that is very resistant to the dominant movement in the opposite direction. In the second period, the attitude of the paws is counter, and it is the inertia of the forequarters that provides at that moment a point of support for the rotation of the hind-quarters.'

Such is the final conclusion of Marey's work on this interesting phenomenon. His explanation is a possible one.

Despite the cat's suppleness and this wonderful rotating power, there are, nonetheless, frequent clinic cases of fracture of the pelvis and reins when a cat slips off the edge of a roof and falls to the ground.

From what height? The majority of cases reveal a rather troubling fact: a cat who jumps easily from the top of a wall ten or so feet high, will be killed, nine times out of ten, if he falls from the sixth floor, but will emerge virtually untouched from a fall of four storeys. Why?

Because very probably the latter gives the exact time that he needs to right himself in space, and also marks the extreme limit of endurance at which, on reaching the ground, the frame and the muscles can undergo the violence of the shock without being broken.

Such are, chosen at random among prejudices and misunderstandings, some of the obscure points that help to keep the cat's behaviour so mysterious. There are numerous others, too.

Do you know that cats have a horror of imitation products? If a cat lies down on a coat, it is either fur or wool; if on a cover, it is either cotton or silk.

It may be that cats, nervous and hypersensitive as they are, can, for reasons of self-protection, detect that little-known antigen found in nylon and other chemical fibres, that antigen to which so many of us, for all our satisfaction with the products themselves, pay a tribute of allergy.

THE CAT HARKS BACK TO EGYPT

While we are on this curious subject of physical sympathies and antipathies, I should like to draw attention to a detail which rather perplexed me when my friend Albert Plécy revealed its existence to me.

All of us, whatever our background, feel instinctive repulsions and attractions, against which nothing can be done. Northern peoples, for example, tend to find garlic sickening and olive oil indigestible; while the true southerner has no taste for cream-clotted pastries, spirits made from grain, or the smoked fish dear to northerners. It is a question of country, habit and favourable or unfavourable biological conditions.

Now cats, all of them – the pedigree ones being just as susceptible as alley cats – are literally overwhelmed by the odour of certain plants that prefer warmer climates: the carnation, the oleander, the mimosa, above all the papyrus, the symbolic plant of Egypt, which grew in such profusion on the banks of the Nile in the time of the Pharaohs.

The plant is familiar, with its narrow pointed leaves whose stalk, a foot or two high, and triangular in section, contains a kind of marrow similar to that of the elder. In our time papyrus is found hardly anywhere except in Sicily, Egypt and, of course, in some florists' shops.

Buy a jar of papyrus and put it on the table. Even a cat who appears to have little interest in smells will go literally mad on discovering this plant. He will breathe it, snuff it with a feverish delight. Wherever you may hide the jar, he will find it. At the sight of it, he will utter little, greedy cries and nibble the leaves as if they were the most appetizing fish or chicken liver. The smell, the taste, the sight of papyrus sets off a kind of delirium in his innermost being – awakens, if you will, certain echoes in his heart.

It appears that Egypt has left her mark on the cat; and he has not forgotten her.

THE CAT IS PROUD RATHER THAN ARROGANT

The cat is proud rather than arrogant; and only his attachment to those he loves can make him depart from his principle, 'Every man for himself,' which people wrongly complain of in him when they ought to admire him the more for it. What more eloquent proof of affection could there be than the fact that he sometimes accepts that familiarity which his nature abhors?

One thinks that one has mastered a cat because he plays with one and seems to give in to one's whims; and then suddenly one sees that he has just made the last concession, the limit beyond which he cannot go without losing face in his own estimation.

One of my friends' cats recently gave me a perfect indication of this. We were all talking together, when slowly he entered the room, with a mixture of reserve and curiosity. He was really quite intrigued, though he made himself look as disdainful and condescending as possible.

I admired his beauty and grace, but restrained myself, as one must do, from making the least advance to him.

'He's as proud as a peacock,' said my friend's wife. 'He can't bear to be touched.'

'Gros Papou a peacock?' cried her husband, astonished. 'Just look here: I can do what I like with him. Watch me turn him over and grab him by the tail. Sometimes I pretend to tear him limb from limb. He loves being bullied.'

Suiting the action to the word, he took Gros Papou in his

arms, stroked him, and then, putting him on the carpet, rolled him over suddenly. This was too much! The cat, with a push of his reins, righted himself and leapt out of reach. Then, with a tremendously dignified air, he left us.

On the threshold he hesitated, turned, and both by way of excusing himself and to emphasize his displeasure at this public humiliation, he gave his master the most eloquent look, an indignant grimace which we all knew the meaning of: a look of outraged modesty that said as clearly as words: 'No! You mustn't do this kind of thing in front of strangers.'

DOES THE CAT FIND A CORNER TO DIE IN?

Can we believe this adage of hunters who, finding a mortally wounded wildcat in a thicket, have initiated the belief: 'Cats look for a hiding-place to die in'? To support this idea, we need in the first place to grant that these animals can think in the abstract and hold such a concept as death; of course they are incapable of this. I have seen too many cats die, both young and old, to believe it.

Free to come and go as they please, the cats who have looked on me as their host have sometimes failed to turn up at mealtime or curfew; but whenever death has touched one of them, I have always found that he has come back home, to the seat of the old armchair, his favourite cushion, or – more affecting still – to my arms. All have died with an evident acceptance, a serenity and overwhelming confidence which, in the face of one's powerlessness to avert the supreme moment, leaves one feeling guilt as well as regret.

I have known only one sort of cats who hide or go to earth when they can no longer defend themselves, attack or fight: it is cats who have been abandoned. They hide like all savage beasts because they have no more strength and above all because they know that they can no longer count on men.

But the others, the happy cats, die without fear or anguish, feeling safe in being loved.

4. MECHANISM

Those people who, knowing virtually nothing about cats, parrot the familiar calumnies and idiotic prejudices and hawk them about everywhere, ought to be subjected to some veterinary teaching – as first originated by Lord de Bourgelet, whose special interest was the horse.

The Academy of Hippology, which he founded at Lyon in 1762, dealt with everything: anatomy, exterior, physiology, psychology, aesthetics, structure. Since then the horse has taken his accepted place in man's scheme of things.

The cat has been treated of by writers only in a poetic vein. As for the experts – in France, at least – they have devoted serious research to him only in recent years. The first book of *Regional Anatomy of the Cat* in the French language dates from 1953. As for psychological works, they are, for sentimental reasons, so very limited and circumspect that, apart from some specialists like artists, breeders and psychologists, those who are interested in the cat are almost never well-informed about him. Conditions being what they are, one can understand how people's interest in him is hampered by so many erroneous ideas.

Clearly it is not by specifying that 'the pulmonary azygous lobe is very short,' or that 'the last sternebrate articulates forward with the one before in such a way as to facilitate oscillation vertically' that we get any further in our knowledge of the cat. We can hardly expect to persuade those indifferent or hostile to him to revise their opinion if we note that his blood corpuscles are oval instead of round.

But what are the canons of cat beauty? What are, physically, chemically, psychically, the secrets of his mechanism?

The cat is all power, elegance, suppleness. He is a serpent on pistons and steel springs. A simple detail about the way he is put together: the invertebrate ligaments are replaced by little bundles of muscles: it would be impossible to find a better concept of elasticity.

Is his body structure elongated or squat? Are his legs long or short? Anyone who has had only glimpses of the cat would hesitate to answer on these points of morphology. For the cat can arch himself at will like the vault of a bridge or can stretch himself out like a fish, and the shortness of his paws depends more on the angular fermature than on the actual length of the 'spokes'.

Well-proportioned, symmetrical, balanced, the cat achieves the ultimate in aesthetic harmony and delicacy.

Have you ever admired a cat's head? 'Short, ovoid, with a relatively diminished face terminated by a blunt muzzle, a cat's head has no internal occipital protuberance or interosseous canals,' says the austere treatises, which add: 'as for his jugular apophyses, they are very badly matched.'

This may be so. But in the eyes of some of us, a cat's head is made for caressing. It should fit in the hollow of a man's hand as snugly as the stone in an apricot or peach, so that one can feel it nuzzling and stirring slowly when the fingers enclose it; and whiskers flattened, it emerges astonishingly unrecognizable and reptilian. Try. There is not a cat standoffish enough not to respond delightedly.

The cat's body? Finely proportioned, combining delicacy and strength, it is part of that beauty so much admired by sculptors and painters. Lying down, sitting, huddled in sphinx position, stretched out or curled up, he is the most felicitous combination of masses and lines. Walking, leaping, or rolling on the ground, his attitudes and gestures are magnificent and wonderful.

This masterpiece of structure, this motor that moves so well – little in the way of analysis of it has been done up to now.

Certainly there is a cat *language*, ranging from the cry of intimidation, the howling of anger or the gentle miaow of mothers, to the rumblings of desire and the sharp sound of pain. Dupont de Nemours believed it possible to distinguish six consonants in this language: the *m, n, g, h, v* and *f*, as well as the vowels used in common with the dog. But then there is also the purr, that regular, muffled sound like an invisible slow-working motor, that so intrigues and fascinates one.

What does the purr signify? Euphoria? Uneasiness? There are cats who, paradoxically enough, purr continuously in the hands of their surgeon.

For a long time the purr remained unaccounted for, until it was discovered that the cat has two glottises, two sorts of vocal cords to which physiologists agree in attributing very different vibrations. In the opinion of Segond, the upper glottis gives the falsetto and the lower one the chest notes. According to Longuet, the lower cords only are of interest phonetically. Landrin, finally, attributing the miaow to the libration of the lower vocal cords, explains the roaring sound as well as the muffled rumblings, and the purr above all, by the undulating vibration of the uppermost cords.

The anatomists, more judicious, have dissected the area section by section, but have abstained from conclusions. So the question will have to be shelved until the day when the cat himself comes forward to speak.

Happily, we are better informed on the functioning of the senses.

To emphasize someone's sharp vision, one says: he has the eyes of a cat, or of a lynx. Does the cat, then, see better than man and the other mammals?

Incontestably he holds the advantage among the predatory animals. As Professor Pierron of the College of France has brought out, the precision with which the carnivores estimate distances is in relation to a *common* field of vision by both eyes, a rather extensive field, and a *total* field, comparatively narrow. Among the herbivorous animals, on the other hand, the common field is very small and, in certain cases, in the horizontal meridian, attains total visibility. Such is the case with the guinea-pig and the elephant.

The cat, with a total field of 287°, as against the common field of 130°, has therefore more visual possibilities than the dog (83°), the lion (120°) and even man: since the latter, with 125° of common vision, has in the horizontal meridian, a total visibility scarcely exceeding 200°.

THE CAT 'SEES' MORE
THAN HE LOOKS AT

To particularize about the cat's remarkable sight, we might ask if he distinguishes forms and colours as we do. Impossible as it is to question animals, experiments on the cat's vision have naturally left some room for uncertainty.

In regard to forms, the cat's image of people and things would seem to be rather blurred, much less sharp than man's. Like the dog, he perceives silhouettes that are more or less cross-hatched, but he does not, for example, see the patterns of a cloth or the folds of a coat.

Do cats distinguish colour better? In order to ascertain this, it would be necessary to take into account a number of different factors: the luminosity of the objects in question, and their smell and mobility. Above all, it would be necessary to establish the degree of attention that the cat brings to bear in such experiments. All these factors can distort the question.

In a general way, however, it is acknowledged that colour-perception does not exist among the nocturnal animals or those with a strong predominance of twilight vision. Now the cat sees very well at night. In the most utter darkness he can thread his way through a game of skittles without upsetting one. His pupillary opening, round when dilated, then closes to be a mere crack; and, wherever he may be, he makes maximum use of the least light which happens to catch an object.

But it must not be overlooked that the cat directs himself and checks his sensations by the long hairs of his eyebrows, lips and cheeks. If then the cat does see colours, it is because the colours emit rays which escape us, but which he can attract: rays which we are in effect aware of when we say: This is a warm red, or a harsh green, or a cold grey.

It is to these hairs that he has recourse when he is not sure of what he has seen. On the other hand, it is to his eyes that he refers ill-defined feelings of alertness transmitted to him by his antennae.

This natural radar can be found elsewhere among animals, and even in man himself. Who knows if men's moustaches did not for a long time play a comparable role?

In animals, the psychosensory functioning, conscious or not, depends so much more on the outside world than on the will of the animal himself. Much more than any actual desire to see, it is the mobility of a being or an object that sets the machinery of the sight working.

The animal receives more than he gives out. His life, being exempt from abstraction, is more concrete than ours. Here is an example taken at random: a man will fear a revolver placed on a table if the barrel points at him. The cat, not knowing that the firearm means danger, is not in the least concerned. But should the gun happen accidentally to fall or even just to shake because of some passing truck outside, immediately this inanimate thing becomes for the cat 'something that moves'. The hairs of his whiskers and eyebrows intercept this wave vibrating in space, transmit it to his brain; and he has scarcely opened his eyes before he is concentrating them fixedly: is it something to be afraid of, or just an unnecessary alarm? Should he get away or stay? In a tenth of a second he has made his decision.

In sum, the cat, in spite of his excellent sight, does not care to trouble himself to look so long as he is not required to do so or there is nothing of especial interest to see. On the other hand, this same apparently indifferent eye can follow, when it wants to, the flight of a midge or a grain of dust in the darkness.

Is this economy of his powers? Or disdain, or discretion? One material fact emerges: the cat preserves the excellent sight of his youth for a very long time; and even among old cats the classic cataract, that more or less seriously afflicts 90 per cent of dogs over the age of eight, is rare, accident apart.

SENSE OF SMELL

And what part does the sense of smell play? Debates on this subject are likewise far from being resolved.

Because the Pharaohs used cats for hunting, it was hastily concluded that the cat's sense of smell must be very remarkable. In reality, this is not the case. The cat takes pleasure in certain strong odours, nitrogenous fermentations. He loves the chlorinated smell of soda, ammonia, fennel and, curiously enough, fresh plaster. Many scents please him, such as carnation, valerian, mint, tuberose and asparagus; while others, like absinthe and above all rue, revolt him. He shows an interest in the stagnant water of vases (rich probably in micro-elements); in papyrus, for reasons we have already explained; in sweat; and in many other odours beside. But he is not really an olfactive creature.

Give him a piece of fish: the smell pleases him and, except very rarely, he accepts it. But offer him some raw beef freshly taken from the refrigerator, and he will approach the meat and smell it, whiskers back. He will even go so far as to brush it absently and circumspectly with his tongue; but that is all. Unless the cat in question is starving or greedy, that is the end of the experiment.

If you want him to deign to accept your offering and eat it, you must place it on the ground, so that he can touch it first with the tip of his nose, immobilize it under his paw and – if it meets with his approval – eat it, his nose down, and shaking his head a little, as wild beasts, liking to feel the warm prey that they have killed under their paw, have always done.

As for our house cats, the odour of cold meat disgusts them, and the odour of mice no longer rouses toms (for all their reputation as killers), except as a reminder of the past.

For a long time I watched a Persian cat whose behaviour in this department was odd. He hunted when he was not hungry, and each time the little drama was played out according to a changeless ritual. Generally on these mornings Lion would turn up his nose at his breakfast. When the clatter of spoons and dishes announced that it was mealtime, he would simply not go to the kitchen. He would get up, go down to the garden or run to the cellar, then come back, a mouse between his teeth, a mouse which he had killed cleanly, without savouring a sadistic pleasure like so many cats who leave their prey just enough life for it to try to get away. He would set the mouse down near his bowl: and then, without ever touching his victim, but given an appetite by its scent, start to eat.

A whim? Not at all. On those days he harkened back to an olfactory-gustative memory echoing from the past.

The cat is enabled to do this by a little organ buried under the pituitary gland and called by anatomists the 'Jacobson organ'. This Jacobson organ enables him to accumulate unconsciously, as human beings do, a reserve of olfactory perceptions, a kind of 'filing-system of odours' unconsciously registered; these, noted and classified once for all, may be quite forgotten or may dog his memory, but are never obliterated.

Dr Hasse is therefore right in asserting that one has only to bring mice to the most delicately nurtured Persians, to reveal the slumbering killer and ratter instincts handed on down the generations.

TASTE

Of the cat's sense of taste, not much has been discovered.

'Their taste', it is declared, 'is secondary to the sense of smell. The cat sniffs, tears at his food, swallows and digests it; but does not taste.'

However, let a cat choose between pure, creamy milk straight from the farm and milk tainted by the city, or offer him stale fish or over-cooked liver or tinned beans, and you will see.

In fact, cats chew very little and very quickly fill up their stomachs, which expand to the maximum and secrete a rich essence of food.

Finally, cats have certain insistent needs which we know little about. They feel hunger, in the psychological sense; pressing hunger for things the lack of which cannot be apparent to us. When these hunger-fits subside, their taste becomes more fastidious.

The cat is far too fastidious to be a glutton; and therefore, not being a gourmand, he is a gourmet!

HEARING

Have you ever tried to wake a sleeping cat? Not just any stray cat, but your own indulged, privileged cat, who shows his affection by choosing to sleep on your jacket in preference to the warmest cover. When you try to wake him, does he stir in the slightest, or twitch a single whisker? You might fire off a cannon without his turning a hair, if the noise is familiar to him.

Is he deaf? Certainly not. Apart from blue-eyed white cats (the true albinos), cats have very acute hearing, an ear so selective that it picks up the least sound of interest to it.

Lenz's observation on this aspect is to the point. One day as he was sleeping in his garden, his cat on his knees, Lenz was suddenly roused by the animal's starting. Surprised, he watched him, and then saw a little mouse scuttling away. It had crossed the sand-covered path where it could hardly have made much noise, and the distance at which the cat had heard it was twenty-five yards. And the cat had been asleep.

But here is a still better example of the exquisitely sensitive hearing of the cat when it is a question of his most cherished needs.

I had accustomed one of my cats to associate a particular noise with his pleasure in a certain dish: it was the sound, inaudible to human ears, of one of those supersonic whistles used in hunting. One day I lost this whistle. Time passed; until eight months later a friend, whom I was bringing home with me, accidentally found the object under a cushion in the car. He asked me some questions about the whistle. To demonstrate, I blew it cautiously two or three times, and then put it in my pocket.

The garage is in the garden. We had climbed two flights when, reaching the landing, I heard a very familiar cry through the door; it was a miaow of hunger. Filou's insistent miaowing, a sharp, prolonged, tyrannical noise, punctuated by deep purrs.

Then we learnt the explanation of the incident. Filou had been sleeping in an armchair when suddenly he was seen to lift his head, listen for a moment, then jump to the floor, run to the kitchen, from the kitchen to the landing, and back to the kitchen, although he had eaten only an hour before.

After eight months, and through the barrier of walls and doors, passages and garden, he had recognized, exactly at the second, that muted whistle which promised his favourite dish.

This was the case with a happy and sated cat. One can imagine then how acute must be the hearing of a cat who is lost and who, with all his senses alerted and his heart beating wildly with panic, creeps on from street to street, hoping to recognize a familiar, reassuring sound.

Picture to yourself the fact that a cat can distinguish at twenty or twenty-two yards two sounds emitted at the same time and separated one from the other by only half a yard. Calculating that this represents a difference in time of .0000028 of a second, you can see that the cat's hearing must inevitably be far superior to the dog's.

Ah, but the cat only hears when he feels like it. Watch him taking his bearings some time; see him sounding the air, as it were, with his ears; then he checks, reflects; and he makes a move only after ascertaining the origin of the noise he hears.

In a similar case, a dog will be precipitate, ready to change direction or pace as necessary. This difference is connected, as Frank W. Lane has shown, with a completely individual hunting-method.

The dog hunts on the ground or into it. No sooner does he smell, see or hear his quarry than he hurls himself after it.

But the cat attacks equally well from the ground or a tree. He must therefore be able to localize all sounds according to their various heights. And then, he advances by leaps, not by uniform running: this is the reason for his taking longer to observe, for his manoeuvring more slowly. He gauges his distances, and only decides to pounce when he is quite certain, and then in absolute silence.

The dog's most important sense is his nose, and the cat's his hearing.

MUSIC AND CATS

A cat, it is said, can distinguish two notes sounded almost simultaneously and a semitone apart, in the scale of sounds audible to man. Here is where the experiment must necessarily end, and where what we call music ends. For a long time it was thought that beyond (or even perhaps this side of) what the human ear can perceive, there were no possible vibrations. By now this mistake has been rectified.

72

In the matter of phonetics and cats, we might make two divisions: that of music and cats, and that of cats and music.

The first division has its share in the egregious misunderstandings between man and the animals. Here is a quotation from an anonymous little work that throws some light on our limited approach:

'Under the pretence that Ovid could have written *Parvous hiando felit,* some lofty minds have named "miaowing" the cat's song and characterize it as frightful, inharmonious and unpleasant. Is this legitimate? Between ourselves, what they call dissonance only indicates their lack of knowledge and taste. We are all too facile in denigrating as "lowing", "howling" or "neighing" sounds whose inter-relationships and beauty are a closed book to us.

'The Egyptians, more enlightened in this, knew that a sound is neither true nor false in itself, and that all depends on the habitual combinations of sound that one is used to acclaiming.

'They knew whether cats, in their own music, passed from one tone to another in the same ratio that we use, and whether cats modified this tone to produce the intervals which we call "commas". They could distinguish the lover and the challenger in a chorus of singing toms; they could appreciate the modulation, simple or indirect, the ease of the transitions, and the sweetness of the sound.

'What we call pejoratively "discord" or "cacophony" just indicates our own limitation, which is both unjust and undiscerning.'

This is a specialist's judgement, of course, but troubling nonetheless. Certainly we cannot help thinking of certain airs of oriental music, or Chinese music, which, because they are unfamiliar to us, we find intolerable after a bit. And then there is Ravel's *Cats*, a little masterpiece of imitative harmony.

Can we affirm, however, that these notes and harmonies correspond to those with which toms rend the air, and which queens appreciate? This brings us to the second aspect of the problem: cats in relation to our music.

The distinguished performer Henry Sauguet has written most informatively on this subject, both as an artist and as a friend of cats:

'I had the good fortune [he wrote in *Chat Beauté*] to grow up with a black-and-white angora cat as my companion; I kept him till my twentieth year. Very early Cody shared in my musical studies. Closeted with me in the room where I practised my scales, he would listen indifferently and without showing boredom. [In any case, the cat is not capable of boredom: he just goes, mentally, elsewhere!] But if I played pieces, he became more interested, indicating his preference by purrs or his dislikes by little cries of discontent.

'For one work, however, one only, he showed attention in the first place, then a real passion. I was sixteen, and I had discovered Debussy. Among his piano pieces that I played, one of them produced an extraordinary effect on my cat: it was *Le Cortège de la Petite Suite*. Listening to it, Cody would roll on the carpet, moaning with joy, then jump on the piano, from there to my knees, and lick my hands, going off and coming back at a terrific gallop when I began to string out those enchanting thirds.

'Dear Cody! His memory is inseparable, for me, from that wonderful page: and I never play it or hear it without it bringing back that light and endearing little presence to me.'

For that matter, Cody was not the only one of the artist's cats to take this curious interest in modern music. There was also Marie-Adelaide-Pompon, who would sit beside the piano and listen to him working away. 'She was impassive, staring fixedly in front of her at the passage of the sounds in space.' Another cat preferred vocal music. Shrill voices, clear ones and coloraturas enchanted her. 'Then she would try to catch the sound in flight with her paw': sounds which, according to M. Sauguet, must have been 'visible, tangible, as it were materialized' for her.

This seems strange. But why shouldn't it be possible? Rabelais spoke of 'words freezing in air', and so was a precursor of the wireless of the future. And would anyone, before Professor von Fritsch had done his patient, incredible research, have believed that bees speak to one another?

Everything is possible, and perhaps we shall learn one day that the ear of the cat is only a controlling organ, and that they can capture resonant vibrations, unhearable by human beings, otherwise than by the agency of their eardrums?

SENSE OF TOUCH

The cat, mistrustful by nature and often by experience, does not count on his eyes alone to see, or on his ears to hear. Like all unbelievers, he has to verify things for himself.

Primarily the cat wants 'to touch'. This sense is his completest and most useful one.

The cat's skin is the intermediary of his contact with the exterior world. On that skin are hairs, the silken hairs of his fur; and in that fur, other hairs, stouter and longer, which nature has wisely planted in the most vulnerable places: whiskers, to detect anything that might hurt the delicate muzzle; eyebrows, to warn and protect the eyes; and at the end of the fur, there is the tip of the nose, as well as the underparts of the toes and paws: all these organs of touch being sharply differentiated.

We have already seen the role that the whiskers and eyebrows play in the cat's seeing. They are better than antennae, and without them the proper functioning of the nervous system would be inconceivable.

To deprive a cat of his whiskers and eyebrows by cutting them off is like depriving a nearly blind man of his hands, or a deaf person of his eyes. Without whiskers and eyebrows, the cleverest cat is reduced to ineffectualness. He loses that astonishing faculty of moving easily among the most fragile knick-knacks. He no longer commands that surprising agility with which, in a third of a second, he can rush into an opening or disappear in a pipe scarcely larger in diameter than his body – which seems almost miraculous to us.

How does he do it? Are we to credit that naïve dictum

which holds that the spread of the whiskers corresponds exactly to the breadth of the body, and that cat uses this 'compass' to estimate if a particular opening is his fit? Undoubtedly, he estimates this mentally. But so many prejudices refuse to be extinguished: these facile analogical explanations handed down through centuries of ignorance.

How many generations of intelligent, educated people have spoken with an equally naïve assurance of the suicide of dogs or the jealousy of tortoises? Each animal lives in its own universe. Each creature has the reactions proper to its species, and its acts are not necessarily linked to the same sensory phenomena that condition the behaviour or activity of another species.

Why should the cat's sense of touch prove an exception to this rule?

Among all creatures, the tactile sense depends on identical principles. Their exploration is therefore functionally the same, whether it be the question of an insect or of a cat. But the latter has such other adjuncts as his nose, or even the antennae-hairs.

Then there are the cushions of each toe, which are as sensitive to heat, cold or roughness as the sole of our foot or the cushion of our fingers. (No one who has seen a cat rubbing some fabric with pleasure or moving with the sureness of a sleep-walker can doubt this.)

Then there is the remarkable fur, so effective a conductor of electricity; it crackles in dry or stormy weather, produces sparks at the least caress, and secretes an unimagined nervous charge. This electric potential has never been measured.

Is it to this that one can attribute the feline's physical resistance, the fact that he is proof against even certain poisonous bites? It is possible. Dr Calmett's work is explicit on this point: like the mongoose and the dormouse, the cat is not susceptible to the snake's venom. Is this immunity natural or acquired? In any case, both domestic and untamed cats show little concern for this danger. This is of course why – unlike the monkeys, to whom it has often been attempted to relate them – cats are not afraid of snakes. The most formidable gorilla, the most adroit chimpanzee, the fiercest orang-outang will tremble before an adder, like a woman at the glimpse of a mouse. Cats are far more uneasy at the sight of a fox-terrier, and we know a cat who lives and plays with two superb pythons ten feet in diameter and over three yards long.

HIS NEUROSES

Estimating in units of caresses, as it were, the power that could be accumulated along a cat's back, an engineer calculates that at least nine thousand million strokes would be necessary to light a seventy-five-watt bulb for a single minute. However, we can allow for imagination in this extraordinary survey. Undoubtedly the cat is not a power station; but he vibrates like, say, a harp or a crystal.

Why does a cat who appears to be tranquillity itself get excited suddenly to the point of losing all control, of spitting his anger and terror, and scratching or biting his master? And if one tries to stop him, he hurls himself against the walls.

Why does the cat feel a horror of being tied down, of feeling himself reduced to powerlessness, when he lets himself be smothered in the most irksome attentions so long as he is left the illusion of being free to run away or defend himself?

The answer is that the cat, sensitive in the extreme, and responding irrationally to the most ordinary excitement, is, neurologically, an abnormal creature.

Whose fault is it?

Like all beings who have for a long time been hounded down, murdered, betrayed, like all those who have suffered in the course of centuries, the cat has become a neuropath only because man's caprices have finally created a state of permanent emotionality in him. It is man who has made the cat into a congenital neuropath.

One female domestic cat out of fifty leads a satisfactory amatory and maternal life; one male in a hundred remains a tom. Condemned to forced celibacy if they have masters, to starvation if they are free, cats have become neuropaths through neuro-glandular troubles, as a result of their most vital instincts being crossed.

To prove this, of course, it would be necessary to alter the cat conversely. We would have to follow and observe thousands of generations of cats. They would have to be allowed to reproduce at will, being given a balanced diet and assured every security.

But it is either too late or too soon. And further, the cat is very far from being a guinea-pig; he does not lend himself readily to research.

A cat has only to be fastened down on an operating table for his normal temperature (about 101·5°) to reach and pass 104°. Should a bottle of ether be uncorked beside him, he will probably salivate for an hour. And if the least dose of morphine (that classic calmant of all other mammals) is injected into him, it will, so far from calming him, aggravate his nervous condition. Finally, all cat-doctors are aware that the sturdiest cat, with the healthiest liver and most regular heartbeat, can die of a syncope in the course of the best-administered anaesthesia.

The cat is a mysterious creature. So much so, that it is difficult to tell where the normal ends and the disturbance begins.

Experimenters have tried to discover this, putting the question in their indirect fashions, provoking reactions, and noting the responses. In the majority of cases, the results confirm or go beyond what observation tells us.

The cat being above all an emotional creature, the experts have set themselves to studying first the manifestations of his affective life. Joys, faithfulness, playfulness, obedience, are easily analysable.

But fear?

The responses to an 'emotional charge' are so different, varying not only with species, but with individuals, as Dr Marcenon has aptly noted. The noise of a passing aeroplane leaves men indifferent in peace-time, but that same noise inspires fear in time of war. At other times, it can frighten timid people without affecting braver ones.

It is the same with animals. Dogs do not behave like cats in similar circumstances. Should one lift a hand against a dog, he dodges; if the threat becomes more definite, he runs away.

The cat will retreat only if he feels himself truly at fault. If not, he begins by flattening himself in terror; then, the first emotion passed, he collects himself and, as if he has found a new strength, he makes a stand, ready to retaliate.

It has been attempted to analyse this phenomenon of fear even further.

Between the cat's fear and that of man there exist psychologically points in common: in both, fear is characterized by an accentuated heart-beat, rapid breathing, a noticeable glycosuria, and, on account of a contraction of the spleen, by a temporary increase of up to 20 per cent in the number of red corpuscles.

At a further level, one notices another phenomenon: a sweat of terror or of anguish, the appearance, in the hollows of the hands or of the paws, of a sudden humidity. It is now possible to measure this curious secretion.

THE CAT HAS PINK FEARS, NOT BLUE ONES

A little bag of cloth or gauze containing two crystals of cobalt blue is placed in the cat's paw, and then some emotion is aroused in him.

At a sudden noise or a dazzling light, sweat appears at first faintly, and the crystal becomes clear blue. At an unexpected whistle, immediately the gauze is tinted lavender. But if a dog is let into the room to leap forward barking, the little bag turns pink.

We know the expression 'to be in a blue funk'; and we know that the faces of Negroes, when they are afraid, become covered with a grey cast. And it is common observation that white people with pink complexions turn pale or green. But after this analysis of the cat's emotional psychosis, the saying will have to be revised: intense fears are really pink, not blue.

*   *   *   *

'Why terrorize a creature', people may say, 'to reach conclusions that are child's play? As for fear, we know all about the troubles it causes.' True enough. But it is only thanks to experiments and research, such as this, that veterinarians can with any certainty combat the neuroses that are at once the charm and the affliction of cats. As a result of experiments like this, adrenalin, calcium and vitamin C are now administered; and it will be possible in the future to help the world's neutered queens and irascible toms.

On account of these experiments, the fierce opponents of what is (wrongly) called vivisection, without knowing the facts, attacked the experts.

IS THERE A CAT-WAVE?

Observation and empirical research, which no control sustains, undoubtedly leaves cats in peace, but also opens the door wide to fables and errors, if not to actual injustice.

As it is, the cat, overpowered by the ignorant and the stupid, suffers from unfavourable prejudices even among intelligent people. It would be easy for his enemies to oppress him even more, if science were not there shedding a little light on the truth.

Before the war the race of Siamese cats was threatened with extinction because an ambiguous news item made people think that Siameses could be carriers of leprosy. And today, because a medical category includes as 'syphilitic' certain cutaneous lesions, anxious correspondents inquire frequently if cats are syphilitic and therefore dangerous. The answer is, emphatically not.

These questions of pathology we shall touch on later. For the moment, let us keep on with these more serious aspects of the cat's enigma.

Does there exist something that might be called a 'cat-wave'?

Many people who are passionate animal-lovers, who could not kill a fly and would fight to defend a strange dog, are *incapable* of taking any interest in a cat. 'I couldn't harm them,' they say in all sincerity, 'but it's a physical thing. The mere idea of just my fingertips brushing a cat's back revolts me, as though it were a question of some slimy monster.'

Henry III of France, it is recorded, fainted at the sight of a cat. Some people are allergic to the cat's hair, and react with an attack of asthma or urticaria to the mere presence of a kitten.

There are even more disturbing cases. Certain women take pleasure in fondling a cat. They keep it in their arms for ten or fifteen minutes, then are seized by a maniac urge to crush it, to squeeze it to death. And the cat, which has meekly suffered everything so far, suddenly begins to struggle, to bristle, until it gets away panic-stricken without even thinking of scratching.

But happily there are also the majority of people who find the contact of a cat soothing, and who feel an inexplicable euphoria in gently stroking its fur, a pleasure comparable to what one feels in gazing absently into a woodfire, or being carried away by music.

A state of balance; a neuro-physiological concordance; the 'cat-wave', then. But of what order? That has not yet been discovered, nor has any means been found of measuring the 'cat-wave'.

DOES THE CAT SENSE THE APPROACH OF DEATH?

'One never bends over a tom', said Francis Jammes, 'without a dumb anguish touching one's heart. Comparing oneself with him, one feels all that separates us and all that links us.'

'All that separates us and all that links us.' To reach some explanation of that emotion, it is certainly worth some study and research, even at the cost of a little remorse.

It is because research has succeeded in inducing and curing eclampsia in females that the rearing of delicate cats has become possible. It is thanks to experiments made with widely different perfumes on cats that, to a great extent, the various troubles that these occasion have been established: the odour of marjoram inspires aggressive crises in cats; eau de cologne and synthetic extracts of flowers make them slaver.

How many cats have been condemned by their best friends, who believed them afflicted with rabies, just because they scratched or simply slavered in these very natural conditions? 'All that separates us and all that links us.'

Misunderstanding is everywhere between the cat and ourselves.

A cat may be sitting in front of a fire gazing into the flames, when suddenly one sees him start up, his eyes dilated, his back arched, ready to leap on an invisible enemy. What is the matter with him? Has he been taken with a sudden congestion, or wakened abruptly from a bad dream, or has he really seen something? Who can tell?

It is said that the cat senses death. There are many cases that raise this question.

A cat has been lying on his master's sickbed, which he has hardly left for several weeks. One evening he disappears abruptly. He will return later, when death has done its work. How did he know of death's approach?

Another cat refuses to leave the coffin of his mistress who was killed two days before in an accident ninety miles away. How has he taken in this concept of death?

What is it that they feel? And what unknown mechanism can set off such attitudes?

To explain the unforeseen accidents of which wild-beast-tamers are sometimes the victims, it has been thought that under the influence of a strong emotion the acidity of the skin can change, causing a modification in the man's habitual odour. This new odour shocks and surprises the beasts, and makes their tamer's image into that of a stranger. Who knows if a short time before death a similar olfactive change is not produced, to which cats are sensitive and which they find unbearable?

One day one of my clients offered me a cat, a young cat several weeks old which had been born in his house and which he had to give away because there were too many. Minou lived happily in our house for a year, then in a few days succumbed to severe meningitis.

And then took place the astonishing coincidence that I can

only relate: the following day I received this note from his original master:

'My dear Doctor, – After a year of silence, you must think me a worthless parent, but I should like to know if you still have Minou, the cat that I gave you then. Just last night, my wife was upset by a prolonged nightmare: she saw him injured on the head and trying vainly to scramble up to us along the façade of the building. To reassure her and to do me a favour, would you please give us some news.'

Now the cat had died that very night, his head wrapped in cold compresses, in a state of extreme agitation that we could not calm.

It is quite a simple story, but without any obvious explanation. Was it coincidence or the natural manifestation of some unknown force?

What, after all, is clairvoyance but the ability of some people to see in space or time events or things which do not reach our senses? And why should animals be deprived of this ability? Why should there not be spiritual or emotional rapports between us, an exchange of psychic waves comparable to that indefinable current called 'sympathy', and of which, with sublime egotism, we have reserved for ourselves the exclusive rights?

It is discovered more and more every day that man is deceived about the true nature of some of his own faculties. What if these are just the remnants of a sensual existence?

What if we are extra-lucid only in those few odd moments when our nervous system, stripped of all intelligent will, approaches more closely the wonderful mechanism, acute and intense, that we call (with what sovereign disdain!) our wretched 'animal nature'!

5. HIS PASSIONS

Animality! What other domestic species on earth has renounced it less than the cat? What creature could pride itself on having sacrificed less servilely to fear, hunger and security?

However – as with the majority of other animals – we have assumed the right to interfere also with the most basic aspects of cats: their love-life. Opposing the inclination of our whims or interests to their desires, we have thwarted their motherhood, controlled their posterity.

Man has never succeeded in subjugating the cat, still less in exploiting him; man compensates for this failure by castrating the cat, destroying his young at birth, opposing a kind of Malthusian obstruction to his deepest instincts. Hunted down and starved for too long, the cat, whom man could make into neither a draught-beast nor a tame hunter nor a dish for the table, the cat, by a biological leap as it were to the defence of the species, seems now to have no desire other than – love itself. Driven back on their sexuality by man's treatment, cats no longer live for anything but passion.

In this category everything is atypical and unpredictable.

Like the bitch, the cow, the mare and almost all other domestic females, the wild beasts are sexually disturbed at fixed periods. They obey a regular activity of the hormones, perfectly controllable. But the female cat is far from regular. After scarcely a few days of respite and calm, she may have a new access of sexual 'frenzy', the rhythm and duration of which cannot be predicted, and the apparent signs of which are variable.

My friend Philibert-Pasha-of-the-straits-of-the-Po, that ex-sailor so named because he was given to me at Port Said by a ship's commander, is a massive, striped cat to whom sex is no longer a concern. Now chance will have it that almost every month he finds himself at the mercy of one Carmen, as thin as he is fat, as little as he is big, as possessed by love as he is stranger to the thing.

And each time the comedy begins, and plays itself out according to a fixed procedure. Carmen starts by creeping up to him and rubbing against his fur, till she has succeeded in distracting him from his nap or his meal. At length Philibert comes to a reluctant decision. He gets up, stretches, yawns, then gives her a bored look. The first day is given up to inno-cent flirtation and touching coquetry. But by the next day Carmen is no longer satisfied with these timid responses. She rolls about, to rouse him. She even insults him a little.

What conditioned reflex, what nervous process then wakens impulses of ardour in Philibert that can only be described as charitable? With little enough conviction he simulates a gal-lantry that scarcely diverts him; wearying of this quickly, he gives up.

By now, though, he has raised such hopes in his friend that she renews her fussing. She supplicates, and this time hurls abuse. In exasperation she falls on him, scratching his face twice, then just collapses into being an unhappy little cat, so noisy about it that Philibert does what he must: he seizes her between his teeth, carries her out by the scruff of the neck, and sets her down in the garden, as a mother would do. Leaving her there on the grass, he about-faces and climbs back to the first floor; here, peaceful at last, he licks himself all over to rid his fur of that odour of female which has soiled him so very absurdly.

The case of good-natured Philibert, transposing what would generally be a combative attitude to the maternal plane, may seem to be a problem of disturbed sexual instinct. But men, too, when their senses are appeased, are capable of the same protective gestures towards a 'sick child' which, whatever its real wants, is happy to be rocked.

Researchers have not yet come to the end of the surprises in the field of the female cat's sexual activity. The mechanism is known, but its causes are less well understood; and the best endocrinologists do not yet know all about the strange impulses of the female cat's nervous centres, nor about her sexual appetites themselves, which are so irregular. The experts are not even in agreement on the point of the first impulse of desire in a cat.

It might be a centrally controlled action of an optohypophysical kind. And then there is the question of the role of the lunar rays in this neuro-hormonal struggle.

Or the first stimulus might be olfactive, as certain researchers, who have initiated the sexual awakening by electric stimulation of the cat's olfactive bulbs, have maintained.

Or then it might be a matter, the reflex once begun, of a kind of general alerting by stages, maintained by the cries, the miaowings, of the creature herself.

The curious can make what they will of each of these hypotheses.

The prescription, meanwhile, is easy, encouraging and harmless: as soon as your cat shows sign of her trouble, shut her into a dark closet, a cupboard, a trunk – anywhere, so long as she can hear nothing and see not the faintest light. Eighty per cent of the time, it appears, this will do the trick with the most ardent of queens.

Well, there is nothing against trying.

Now as to the males. It must be noted that in male cats – the celibate ones, that is – the echo of the sexual instinct is far less tyrannical. And there are charming toms who are just as gentle and affectionate as neuters. But should there come to their ears, through dividing walls and streets, the cry of an importunate female, even the most civilized toms will struggle to get back to the world of love and amatory combats.

And these latter know no quarter. They have their habitual ceremonial: from the combat of challenge, to the struggle for admission, succeeded by that of expulsion, or the 'ordeal of the rivals'. In the end, strategy and diplomacy are dropped: there is still intimidation, but courage is what really counts, and the all-important factor of being last to win the match and thus enabled to enjoy the fruits of victory in peace.

Among cats at large, only after the strongest has put all the others to flight do the couple, left alone at last, abandon themselves to love-making and its joys.

But 'joys' is not perhaps the right word, when one comprehends why the climax rends from the hardiest such a cry of pain. The male? A Malayan kriss, painfully rough, so that the completion of the act is a liberation.

So much for the physical aspect. Now what about the psychic?

'If you want to be a psychological novelist and write about human beings, the best thing you can do is to keep a pair of cats,' wrote Aldous Huxley in *Music at Night*. Nothing could be truer. Apart from anatomical detail, the daily life of a cat couple is astonishingly like that of a human husband and wife.

Of all the other mammals, cats alone, like humans, live only for love. Their closest cousins, the lions and tigers, go through long periods that can be described as asexual, in the course of which each will hunt for himself, eat, sleep, live only for himself; and it is the same with wild-cats.

The domestic cat-couple never know this respite. A male

and a female who live under the same roof are truly married. Because – without one knowing exactly why – she can need her male at any moment; and because he cannot fail to rejoin her at once, they are bound together at least as much as are the husband and wife in a human marriage.

Cat-lovers ought not to be satisfied with having one cat only. Keep a couple; watch their daily life together. Everything is there, all the ingredients of love: our pride and weaknesses, our despair and joys, our selfishness, generosities, resentments and jealousies.

Resentments and jealousies? Impossible to doubt the existence of these, after having seen a female cat welcome home her vagabond mate who has been absent for three days. Sniffing his hair, she gets the odour of other females, and hurls herself claws first on this ingrate. And the poor guilty husband, with a resigned air and half-closed eyes, submits without flinching from his punishment. Or the sated tom will lick his mistress, who is now to be a mother, with little strokes of his tongue, while she assumes the air of a gratified princess.

And just as in human love there are some elements of behaviour that surprise and disconcert, so in the sexual psychology of the cat there are points of unreason where scientific accuracy itself must lose the thread.

Let us return to Philibert, that neutered cat who let himself be knocked about, flown at, martyrized by an irascible Carmen, whom he treated with such indulgent gentleness. One evening Carmen disappeared. She returned five days later, starving, battered, but content. Then for the first time Philibert smelled her, distinguished the scent of a male, and gave her such a walloping that since then she is all submissiveness and self-effacement, having altered her role from that of demanding, dominating bacchanalian to the discreetest, most respectful and resigned of companions.

The famous cat-feeding lady of Rome . . .
. . . and a modern-day St Francis

The same family. Tabby (above) and tiger cubs (below).

These two pedigree Abyssinian kittens will one day have to endure twice-weekly baths as stoically as Colyum Marcus (below), champion of champions

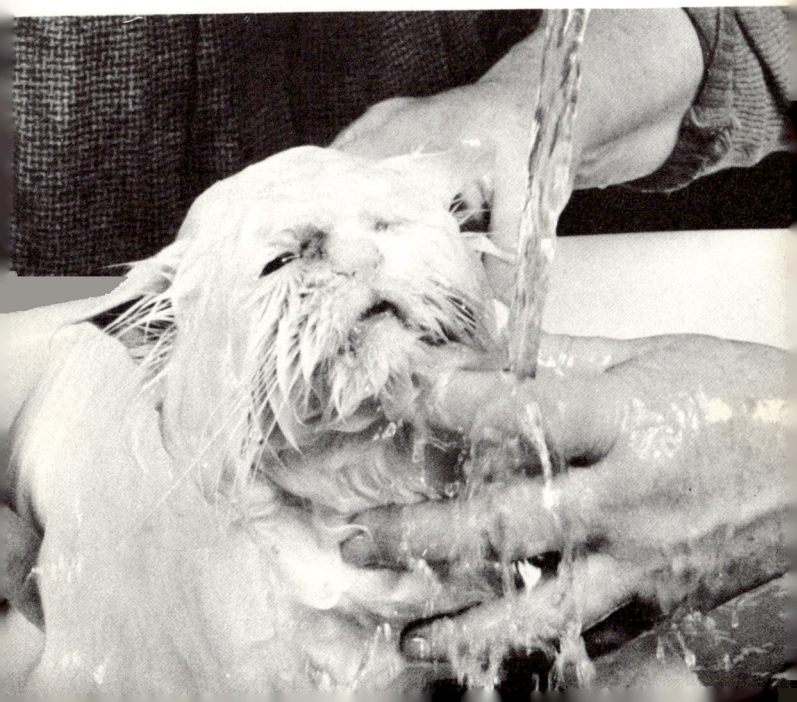

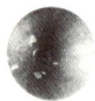

Linked to sexual activity, of which it should always be the normal fruition, the cat's maternal instinct is the more insistent for being thwarted more often than desire itself is.

No other female attends with more fervour to the call of maternity, or submits more passionately to it. None obeys it with more 'intelligent abnegation'; one cannot help using such a phrase, when one knows to what extent the cat is slave to her maternity.

The entire United States press related the odyssey of that American cat who, being about to give birth, was looking for a safe retreat. The chance of her search having led to the packing workshop of a car factory in Detroit, she let herself be locked in there, then at night crept into a case generously heaped with straw, and waited.

The next day the case was hoisted aboard a large ship leaving for Egypt. It contained motors destined for a Cairo garage.

Forty days later, after being unloaded at Alexandria, the case was sent on by train and truck, and reached its destination.

And on the morning of the forty-second day, a workman finally un-nailed it. What was his astonishment to see emerging from the sawdust, emaciated and with half-closed eyes, a cat and her four babies, four kittens five weeks old, which she had fed, cleaned and brought up miraculously.

Forty-two days without food or water! Five weeks in an inferno.

How had she held out? How had she been able to survive? There she was. She had pushed aside the straw and the sawdust, hollowed out a nest, and, out of axle-grease and lubricating oil and also her own blood, had made milk, all the milk that was needed.

An incredible performance, when one thinks of the mineral losses which the best-fed cats suffer in the course of gestation and nursing. Nature draws on the mother's supply of calcium to build the little skeletons; and this precious calcium is built up with the help of three definite factors: animal fat, vitamin D and light.

Forty-two days in the dark, without liquid and almost without nourishment. Only a cat could achieve such a thing.

In a similar plight, many other animal mothers would have killed and eaten their young one by one, for their own subsistence. But the cat is not the rabbit. She strives for the impossible; and only death can release her when, the calcium in her blood coming abruptly to low ebb, she suffers the terrors of eclampsia and its spasms.

We must be impartial, and not make a heroine of the cat. But then, in all fairness, we must not rank other mothers higher than her; as they could not possibly be less 'animal' or more 'spiritual' in their motherhood.

Little by little, we shall get to the bottom of this disturbing maternal *instinct* which, among most felines, comes so close to being a *feeling*.

There is less and less tendency today to judge the merits of mothers. There are no good or bad mothers. There are females whose hormone balance is perfect, and others in whom it is patently disturbed. If this knowledge minimizes feats of motherhood, it also excuses failings.

In dealing with the question of maternal functions, a simple detail is often overlooked: the mother is not alone. There are also the babies. Already in gestation the infants play a determining part, in the progressive awakening of maternal behaviour which they condition. The birth accomplished, their role will become even more important: their presence alone suffices to inspire the maternal tenderness or at least to set the attachment in motion.

Do animals bring consciousness to this emotional behaviour? Is it discernment or just blind propensity?

The American school of thought cited above says that the instinct is fixed: the new-born infants arouse the maternal instinct in a mother, not because they are *her* babies, but because they are new-born babies.

How? What is the mechanism of this? A French researcher

has demonstrated it. This stimulus, according to C. P. Leblond, is a question merely of the presence of magnesium in the organism. Mothers whose diet contains no magnesium bring perfectly normal offspring into the world, but they pay their children no more attention than another female, say a wet nurse, would pay them.

What is to be concluded from this scientific data, if not that the maternal instinct is, as Professor Rémy Colin wrote, 'a latent power of hormonal origin which permits certain automatic actions to take place *at the sight of* new-born animals'? Sensibly, however, this endocrinologist does not exclude the emotional contraction. He admits that certain females are less subject than others to the tyranny of their hormones, and that that instinctive behaviour, 'still undeveloped and uncertain, prefigures the splendid reality called "maternal love".'

Feeling or mechanism? Comprehension or automatism? How can we determine the exact boundaries? And how can we attribute to instinct alone so many cases of daily observation where mother-cats show such initiative as to silence the strictest Cartesian?

KITTENS

Marvelling, curious about everything, with a psychic pliancy exceeding that of the puppy, the baby cat is one of the most disarming and engaging sights in the animal world.

The newly-born kitten, however, is not beautiful. Wet, dirty, scratched, he grimaces like a human baby; but at the end of an hour, he has taken shape. In ten days' time he will open his eyes; and in a month, he will be a masterpiece.

It is much the same with a puppy, of course. But at two months, a cat is far more precocious than a baby dog of the same age. His reflexes are more rapid; his sensitivity is keener. Taking into account that all animals act by association of sensation, it is a striking fact that the sense activity of kittens and their immediate responses entail a different behaviour from that of the human baby or puppy.

A human baby will put everything that he can get hold of

in his mouth. The puppy will smell anything that his paw happens to light on. The former is a gustative, the latter an olfactive, creature.

The kitten, who is exclusively neither the one nor the other, is primarily a visual creature. He wants to see everything. His innocence, his curiosity about life are implicit in the transparent gaze of his large eyes. And what could be more confiding than his impertinent enthusiasm to draw you into his games?

Even the enemies of cats cannot gainsay this charm. In certain circumstances the dog himself is disarmed by it.

The newspapers have made much of a recent example of such solidarity. The chief actor and witness in the case was a decent young man whose roughness was partially assumed no doubt to prevent his being suspected of mawkishness or lying.

On the edge of a national highway, a watch-dog and a kitten were playing a game of war, in front of their master's farm. The kitten would attack the big dog; and the latter, pretending anger, would bring down his fragile adversary, throwing himself on him as though to disembowel him. Then the little cat would simulate terror, but at the first moment's respite would make off at a gallop, only to return and resume the pretended battle straight away.

The game, the race and pursuit, had brought the two animals, without their being aware of it, into the very middle of the road, when suddenly an enormous truck appeared, a hundred yards away. The noise of the horn, blasting at them, although still distant, was enough to alert the dog, who got out of the way with one bound. The kitten, surprised and bewildered at first, was then completely frozen by the noise of the blaring horn and the thunder-like approach of the truck. Rooted to the spot, shrinking into himself, his eyes closed, he waited.

For what? Not death; not even pain, which he could not possibly foresee. He was waiting for nothing. It was simply that the wonderful mechanism had ceased to function. (Among human beings, too, fear can 'paralyse'.) Another half-minute, and the truck would be upon him.

With a screech of brakes, the truck jolted to a stop. The

driver could not help braking when he saw this extraordinary sight: the big dog, changing his mind, had come back at a gallop, leapt into the road, seized the helpless kitten and was carrying him between his jaws to the other side of the embankment.

Can this be called a feat? A number of interpretations can be placed on such behaviour. Did the dog have a real desire to save his friend *in extremis*? Or, more prosaically, was it just a matter of reflex of the property instinct; a sudden and selfish concern to recover the toy, the living toy which he had briefly forgotten in his own flight? Or was it a gesture simply echoing the maternal, which is as strong in the male as the female when young are in danger? All points of view are arguable, even a more high-flown, poetical one.

The driver of the truck explained himself: 'I braked sharply, in spite of the heavy weight of my load, and I didn't understand why. As for cats, one runs over a lot of them that one could avoid, I suppose; but this one was too young and too pretty. Why did I brake just automatically? I don't know.'

So much for the indifferent, those who can hardly be said to be blinded by their love for cats. As for the others, cat-lovers past and present, they would probably agree that a kitten's mischievousness constitutes its chief charm. There could be no better distraction for people who have lost their illusions about human beings.

III

Towards the Future

By turns branded and cosseted, worshipped or cursed, according to the people and the century, the cat has reached a new turning in his history.

His destiny is marked with cruel trials. What forfeit has he yet to pay, in order to be taken notice of or allowed to disappear?

The time is not so remote when, to protect châteaux against fire and destruction, cats were walled up alive between the stones or in the lime.

Many of these mummified corpses were discovered in the course of the last war when, by the fortunes of attack, violent bombing of fortresses and ramparts knocked down hitherto indestructible monuments.

Preserved, sheltered from the air and totally dried up, their claws shrivelled, their jaws open in despair, the body contracted to the utmost, these cats proclaimed the indignation of their suffering across the centuries. They proclaimed the horrible death imposed on them by beings who professed to believe in God and to serve Him.

How have we progressed today?

Selfishness has succeeded ignorance, fear of God has given way to stupidity, and a swagger has replaced the old fear.

Nothing has changed.

6. HIS MARTYRDOM

It is no longer the fashion to boil cats in oil or to crucify them. The flames no longer mount around them suddenly, as used to happen on the solstices of St John, when through the bars of a reddened cage their melting bodies would feed the embers. But the cat's martyrdom is not yet over.

Individual crimes against cats? The present day abounds in them; regularly the law courts are crowded with them: with cases of cats saturated with petrol and turned into howling torches ('for fun'), of cats under whose feet sulphuric acid has been sprinkled ('to make them dance') – and others equally horrible and revolting, such as the following. Impelled by hunger, a cat entered a restaurant in Maubeuge one evening. The proprietor, catching sight of it under a table, seized it and in cold blood disembowelled it with one slash of his knife, before the shocked eyes of the diners. Two of them, horrified, attempted to intervene, but he turned on them like someone possessed. Sentenced by the Thirteenth Correctional Court to pay 1500 francs fine in respect of the Grammont Law (what a paltry punishment!) he had the impudence to file an appeal. The sentence was happily confirmed.

Encouraged by the weakness of the laws, these murders and other comparable tragedies take place in sets.

Faced with a decrease in game animals (for reasons that cannot be gone into here: disease, traps, poaching), the hunting world became upset. It looked about for something to blame. So one day the cat (domestic and stray) was officially decreed the enemy of rabbits, hares, partridges, ducks and quail, although these creatures have never ceased to co-exist with cats since the beginning of the world.

The cat was the scapegoat; a pogrom began in broad daylight, as it were. Here are some apposite lines from a hunting journal:

'All means are valid for the destruction of the cat! You will find that he can sustain gunshot wounds, and we advise shooting him with a good No. 5 cartridge. Never spare one of these creatures, whenever you meet one in the course of a hunt or a tour of inspection. In addition to which, all dogs, with a little encouragement, will chase them. It must be remembered that a tom never gives rise to a long chase; he will prefer to climb a tree from where, believing himself safe, he will defy his adversaries – until the fatal shot.

'Poison can also be used. Strychnine or cyanide should be given in pellets of meat, mixed with offal, or put in fish. The bait should be left near a lane habitually frequented by cats, or at the edge of a track. Cats' eating habits must be taken into account: they will smell the bait first and swallow it only in very small mouthfuls. It should be so prepared that when he snatches it up, the contact will break the camouflaged phial, the contents of which will run down his throat. Provide a solid surrounding immediately round the bait, as the cat will tend to try and get at it by passing his paw through the enclosure.

'In a wood he will prefer clean, dry tracks. A well-placed trap or box set out at the edge of the road will catch him easily. To attract him, the trap or the interior of the box should be rubbed with valerian root, the odour of which he appears to like.

'When you find a cat caught in the trap, kill him instantly. Do not try to touch him, as he will scream, spit and claw. Despite the joy of this success(!) it is inhuman to let the victim suffer; a few strong blows with a stick on his muzzle will finish him. But the best method of destruction is undoubtedly shooting, although it rather damages (!?) the beast. For a dead cat has this use: he makes first-class fox bait.

'Kill stray cats unsparingly! . . .'

Nothing could be more brutally, as well as more unconsciously, sincere. But this kind of murder-appeal is not to be satisfied with such lurid prose. It wants sanctions, to appease people's consciences; or at least the plea of civic responsibility. It needs to hide behind legal excuses.

CATS IN TOWNS AND IN WOODS

The excuse was sought, and found: the 'hunting' cat was discovered.

In November 1949 there was published in France an Order in Council which was, at the very least, thoughtless. On the signer himself it brought such uneasiness that he resigned that same evening (for another reason, the Press stated; but we know better).

By the terms of this Order it was henceforth permitted, if not recommended, to shoot stray cats and, by inference, all domestic cats encountered more than two hundred yards from a house.

It can readily be imagined how this regulation was abused. It was the St Bartholomew massacre of rural cats, of peaceful, well-fed toms who ventured to chase a butterfly near the vicarage garden or to sleep on the sunny old wall two hundred yards from their farm. Over-zealous gamekeepers were incited by it to action against all 'hunting' cats (in most cases the cats were hunting love, not rabbits). And so it went on.

However, all mayors in France must know that the Order, which has since been annulled before the Council of State, is now illegal. Thus anyone who deliberately kills a domestic cat is legally guilty of breaking the Grammont Law, and financially responsible for the damage, material and moral, that his shot may have caused.

But if bad news travels quickly, good news lags behind. On the actual evening following the issue of the Order, the enemies of cats began their slaughter.

Those offenders who are prosecuted do not hesitate to declare their good faith. Certain ones even take pride in the number of their victims. 'The Law is on our side,' they say.

I repeat here for their benefit that this is not true.

Do 'hunting' cats still exist? Do we understand by that term cats of the domestic types which have resumed and kept the state of liberty through successive generations? And if these exist, how are we to distinguish them from the *Felis Sylvestris*, the wild cat which existed in Europe long before the cat derived from Egypt and which had no connection with the origin of the domestic cat?

Dr Deriaz is very sceptical on this subject: 'Of the cats found in various collections under the label of "wild cat", one in two is authentic; and then how can one be sure even of that one, since it is dead?'

The characteristics of the wild cat and of the 'hunting' cat are very similar: the same bone structure, the same fur, claws, teeth and tail. A careful examination can perhaps differentiate the under-part of the paws: supple, greyish and more flexible in the cat that was formerly domestic; and a drier and invariably black sole in the real sylvan cat. All this remains imprecise, however.

With cats captured alive, the difference is more obvious. The sylvan cat is really savage in so far as one cannot tame him. In zoos (where he is rare) he seeks out darkness, hiding for whole days. He will take his food directly from no one, and, to our knowledge, the cats called wild have never reproduced in captivity.

Therefore we do not know much about his reproductive processes, the period of gestation, or the natural behaviour in general of this golden-eyed, chubby-faced feline; and this is a pity. A systematic study of him could contribute to solving the mystery of the domestic cat's emergence in Africa.

A more thorough knowledge of the wild cat might even have prevented his extermination. After all, Nature is a complete whole within which a balance is to be found. There are a hundred examples to prove this. If the destruction, often blindly undertaken, of so many predatory animals had not been going on for ten years, the thousands of rabbits affected by myxomatosis would not have spread the disease so easily. And it may be that the lynx and wild cat are equally necessary in the scheme of Creation.

One thing at least is certain: where lions, zebras and antelopes live unmolested, there are still antelopes and zebras. Where man has intervened, there are no longer antelopes or zebras or lions.

CATS IN TOWNS AND GARDENS

But to return to the domestic cat. The cat's greatest martyrdom is not that of the sylvan wild cat or even of the semi-free cats in villages. These latter, after all, belong to someone, can be protected and manage to subsist.

The real martyrdom of cats is that of strays in towns, who live a hole-and-corner existence around fences and gardens.

To what extent are these the victims of human selfishness? There are the cats put out on the streets because their owners are going on holiday; there are those who, kept with their mother – just for her milk – are abandoned when they grow up: all those cats who, weary of hiding all day, of avoiding cars, dogs and brutal people, come together instinctively to find refuge in the meagre thickets of public parks, behind fences in empty lots or houses in construction. Then, with the coming of winter, how ever do they bear the cold, rain and hunger?

Then people condemn them for their passionate natures, for multiplying, for complicating the problem by being prolific. It is the same as with those underprivileged peoples

(Hindu, Chinese or Negro) who can have no more imperious instinct on earth than that of reproduction. They can hardly be blamed for a biological urge forcing them to create life to put away death.

These cats are blamed for being mistrustful and savage. 'The real cats who wander the streets', said Picasso, 'have nothing in common with the cats one sees in houses. They have bristling fur and run like demons. If they look at you, it is as though they are about to leap at your face and scratch out your eyes. The cat of the suburb is a wild beast.'

And how could this outlaw be other than a terrorist?

What do they eat, these thousands of city cats belonging to no one? On good days, perhaps some greasy paper, a few insects and, here and there, a bird or a rat stupid enough to cross their miserable path. Then, what do they eat when the birds have long since migrated, when the snow lies thick on the ground, and those kind providers who help them to keep just alive become rare?

In Paris, of course, as in all French cities, there are decent people, often badly off themselves, who have to hide as though doing something shameful from the inhuman keepers of the squares, when they come to murmur some words of affection to those anonymous cats, to offer them a caress, to bring them the necessary minimum, as if trying to excuse in the eyes of these intelligent creatures humanity's ugliness.

PARIS, BUCHENWALD OF CATS

Impossible to recount the daily, obscure little dramas of these starved wretches. The bloody battles; the entire weeks spent in waiting; the victories that have to be won for the right or the boldness to be among the five or six privileged to fall on any edible rubbish and carry it off jealously as if it were the most wonderful prize. What becomes of the old, the injured, the mangy and the sick among them?

One day one of these Samaritans (whom foolish and worthless people make sport of when they ought by rights to admire them) managed to get hold of a grey cat whom she had noticed for the last week half-buried under a pile of leaves. This living skeleton had a split eye and a wound crawling with worms. She looked after him and cured him. The pus-filled eye had to be enucleated and drained, and the infected back injury had to be stitched three times. A month later, healed, washed, tamed and purring with gratitude, this old grey cat had become a big and stout *white* tom.

But for one such marvellous escape from suffering, how many others die of spade-blows that break their bones and fracture their skull, or squirm with agony in traps, or, suffering from the effects of bait containing strychnine, go rigid with the most frightful spasms? How many innocent kittens and delicate cats choked with pleurisy or exhausted by constant diarrhoea surrender their little lives without understanding what curse pursues their breed, which wants only gentleness and peace?

Why are there two different scales? Stray dogs are much less unfortunate. In towns especially they know how to get about, adapt and defend themselves, and if they happen to be caught, poisoned, they are impounded and put to sleep, their troubles quickly over. According to law a stray dog is necessarily suspect of having rabies, and on this account is put down. (France has found no better way of lessening the danger of this virus which for centuries has made men tremble. The old terror of it still persists.)

Why should cats not be destroyed also?

And I beg the partisans of these unfortunate outcasts to understand me. Why shouldn't many of these wretched cats be put down for the same preventive reasons?

This illustrates once more the particular ill-fortune of the species. If ownerless cats are not put down more often, it is simply because there are not all the facilities for capturing them that make the catching and putting to sleep of a dog a simple formality.

The dog still trusts man. A cat will bite and scratch and with a couple of bounds be out of reach.

Very well; so the matter is allowed to rest. However, it would not be impossible to use a last bait. Why not offer these starving creatures some unlooked-for food which could contain an opiate, a dose of anaesthetic strong enough to make it possible (without any injury to the person) to get hold of them and free them painlessly from their troubles?

It is time to put an end to this vile nightmare of which countless decent people are ignorant. And it is a question of a creature whose entire organism is only vibrations, a creature neither tame nor savage, but condemned by our blind selfishness, in the heart of a civilized city, to a lot which no other animal species in the world has ever known: to die of cold, hunger or fear, without other respite than that of an ephemeral embrace, itself wrung from his fellow sufferers, and at what a price!

It is, however, a problem that will have to be solved one day, in one sense or another: the day when some epidemic will attack the cat – and man; or the day when the cat will be the only bulwark against some plague brought by rats.

Simple figures can show the inestimable value that these creatures, despised as they are, can have for modern civilization.

In America, it is estimated, there still exist 300 million rats which yearly destroy 600 million dollars worth of food. Thus there are nearly two rats and twenty mice per person. And, as the Egyptians themselves noted, what the rat does not eat he destroys, and what he does not destroy he fouls.

In the richest countries, the most civilized cities of today, each of us spends two days of his life in working to feed the rats. In Europe depredations by rats in 1955 cost half the value of the Marshall Plan in grain, despite all the exterminating campaigns and all the poisons. What other force can oppose the rat?

There remains the cat: during thousands of years, and all over the world, the cat has proved himself. If cats which hunt rats are useful (and all the starving ones are potential ratters), so-called civilized peoples should not only tolerate them but also feed and protect them.

But these peoples couldn't care less, as can be judged from this report in *Aux Ecoutes*:

In the Bibliotheque Nationale Paris owns the most precious works, priceless bindings and manuscripts amounting to a treasure. To combat the rats, who of course love books, the official budget provides for one single cat, allotting it a sum of thirty francs a year. Thirty francs a year, and one single cat! These are official figures. In reality more than twenty-five cats carry out this service, and it is actually the employees who at their own expense maintain these precious defenders of our wealth.

Let us have done with this. If cats are useless and undesirable parasites, then there is no excuse for allowing them to continue to suffer neglect and to run the risk of becoming game-animals in the future.

The Grammont Law? Of what use is it? It is as effective as a toy sword against the sadists, slaughterers and poisoners of cats in squares or against the authorities responsible for these massacres.

A light sentence here and there? An official reprimand? And tacit absolution, complicity.

What is the good? The drama has to be considered on a higher level; and since cats are attracting notice today for other reasons than pity, since the 'feline sport' is spreading throughout the world, it is on this level of zoo-technical reproduction that we can effectively work.

Only the breeder of pedigree cats can make this outlaw of interest in a material sense and give him a material value. Only the breeding of selected cats – whether for utilitarian or sentimental reasons – can save the cat.

7. HIS LAST CHANCE: FELINOTECHNICS

It has been said often enough that history repeats itself eternally. All things considered, what is true of human destiny is not inapplicable to the history of animals.

Why did the dog become so involved in our lives that he is indispensable to us? Quite simply because in the first place man needed to hunt for a living. The genuine hunt was born on the day when the dog made it possible, the day when the prehistoric dog and man joined up to track, kill or capture their game more quickly and surely.

The rest was only civilization, progress, the birth of venery, the employment of firearms, the abolition of privileges, the democratizing of the hunt, the foundation of the dog cult. In this way the pure-bred dog was born.

The dog went on, in various guises (as fighters or hunters, watchdogs, show dogs, pets, etc.), to win a worldly place for himself that every successive generation has confirmed.

Why has the cat not profited by the same circumstances?

There is no need to decide here on the question of whether the alley cat is handsomer, more intelligent, engaging and useful than the pedigree cat; but one thing is clear: no one has ever seen a show champion, whether Burmese or cream-coloured Persian, die of hunger, cold or misery.

If then in the not-so-distant future only pure-bred cats are to be protected, cared for, happy, then let us say frankly: it would be best for the old alley cat to disappear quietly, and let the pedigree cat survive thereafter.

8. PRINCIPAL
DEFINITIVE BREEDS

As always in the matter of animal-rearing, the English led the way. The first cat show, in 1871 in London's Crystal Palace, brought together over three hundred entries.

It was only in 1926 in France that the present author, as founder and secretary-general of the Central Feline Society, organized at the Wagram Hall in Paris, under the presidency of Dr Lépinay and Mme Marcelle Adam and with the collaboration of some Parisian veterinary surgeons, the first public showing of specially bred cats.

The success of this initial attempt surpassed all hopes. Speedily the example was followed with the founding of the Cat Club of Paris (Mlle Tzaut) and the Cat Club of Champagne (Mme de Tassigny and M Charles Fournier).

So the movement was launched. Thanks to the efforts of enlightened amateurs, such points as the eye-colour of Angora cats or the length of tail in a Siamese became matters of absorbing interest.

As a matter of fact, of the other breeds apart from these two, only the grey Chartreux and the white-gloved Burmese were known, and just barely, at that time. This was very inadequate. Moreover, there were too few examples of these known breeds to ensure enough participants in the subsequent shows. So the common cat was given his patent of nobility. As well be hanged for a sheep as a lamb: he became the 'European cat'.

Since then we have never looked back.

Today the French Feline Federation, founded by M Guingand, includes some fifteen special clubs. The International Feline Federation, which owes a debt to the example of France, musters the best breeders and fanciers of pedigree cats in Belgium, Holland, Switzerland, Denmark, Sweden, Norway, Italy, Austria, Germany, etc.

The rearing and selling of cats and the dependent industries or activities (pharmaceutical products, medicine, transport, food, etc.) account for a figure of several tens of milliards of francs every year.

Cats have their specialist doctors. They have their periodicals and clubs, their hygienists, poets, sculptors and painters. As for their supporters, they belong to every social class, without distinction; and international champions as often originate in the porter's basement as in the film star's boudoir. Out of this friendly competition are born breeds that are more and more closely defined, more and more characterized according to body structure, appearance and aptitudes: breeds to please every taste.

In less than a quarter of a century fanciers have agreed and acknowledged officially that there are long-haired and short-haired cats.

Among the former are Persians, which can be: blue, white (with either blue or orange eyes), black, cream-coloured, russet, bluish-cream, smoke-grey, tortoise-shell and white, red-brown tabby, brown tabby, silver tabby or chinchilla.

Apart from Persians, this category includes Burmans and Kmers.

The second group, short-haired cats, comprises: Chartreux (blue-grey), Russian blues, Abyssinians, Manx cats, Burmese, Siamese, and the ever-increasing range of Europeans: white, cream-coloured, tortoise-shell and white, mottled, striped and ringed.

In fifty years' time, what will remain of this eclectic register? Will breeds like the Kmer, bred from Siameses and Persians, revert to one or other original breed? And will the pseudo-

Burmese cat, which comes of a Siamese father and an unknown mother, succeed in establishing itself? Not that it is of much consequence. These two breeds are bound to have stirred up a number of controversies all the same, and the most important result – to arouse interest on behalf of all cats – will have been achieved.

A PAGE FROM THE 'ZOOTECHNICAL' NOTEBOOK

It is of greater interest to discover how the various breeds came into being or were founded.

The old-fashioned theory, according to which every type of domestic animal must have a wild ancestor, has been long since discarded, and we do not even know, it must be remembered, where the cat came from.

Therefore it is as tricky to affirm that the Siamese or Abyssinian is definitely the prototype of the first cats, as to maintain the prehistoric existence of a long-haired feline from which the Persian cat of today must be derived.

Whether it is a question of the colour of the coat, length of hair, the shape of the head, or of height or weight, the particularities of a breed are due to changes that have occurred in the sexual cell, in the chromosomes and in the genes harboured by these chromosomes.

One day a mutation appears, accidental or induced, establishes itself, and a breed is born, if the characteristics are sufficiently evident and distinct to differentiate it from others of the same species.

Certainly there are not the multiform varieties of cats as of dogs – from the Pekingese to the St Bernard, for example.

Briefly, cats fall into two categories:

First, the long-lined ones, slender, elegantly proportioned, with long muscles and a head describing a triangle; the most prevalent type here is the Siamese.

Second, the short-lined, short, thick-set, squat ones, with a massive, round and at the same time square head: the Persian cat is the most common example.

Within these two categories, there are two kinds of coat, short-haired or long-haired (this latter being regarded as connected with a recessive gene); and within these two classifications by coat, a whole register which the science of genetics is learning a good deal about, and to which Dr Senet, in the course of zootechnics of the Ecole d'Alfort and the Institute of Agronomic Research, has devoted the most extensive study.

I shall not involve the reader in the technical details of a work beyond the scope of this book. The chief fact is that the gene-structure of cats contains at least ten genes of coloration, of which some can determine such or such a coat by themselves, while others depend on adjoining genes to produce visible effects.

If, for example, white is dominant, it will produce a completely white coat, whatever genes are present. If it is recessive (as is most frequently the case), it can bring about a widely different range of coats.

The design of the markings is itself of infinite variety: ringed, spotted, striped, etc.

Breeders denote by the name of 'tabby' the characteristic of a striped or spotted coat which is more or less irregular but always distinctly delineated against a clear, homogeneous background. So there are European tabbies, Persian tabbies, etc. The English have altered the etymology of this word from the Spanish.

In the language of Cervantes the word *tabi* is defined by the Academy dictionary as follows: a silken cloth resembling watered silk. *Tabi* does not signify the quality of the cloth here, but the designs in the texture reminiscent of the movement of waves or water, as C. Sanz Egana very rightly pointed out. The word should therefore be written 'tabi', although the Iberian expression is not actually used in Spain to designate the common cat, which is known there as *gato Romano* or Roman cat.

For the uninitiated, who easily confuse these two types of tabbies, we can specify that the striped cat has a single dorsal stripe and some transverse ones, while the ringed cat has three parallel dorsal stripes and marble markings more or less ringed or spiral on the rest of the body.

To discover what physio-chemical mechanism and what geographical distribution account for ringed or striped cats, it would be necessary to set up regional collecting centres and trace cats' evolution through successive generations. What is known is that russet and black (which are genes of increase) are connected with gender: hence bi-coloured males are rare and tri-coloured males even rarer, to the extent that if one happens to see a cat whose coat contains white, yellow and black, the chances are ninety-eight out of a hundred that it is a female.

Other factors equally affect the coat: diet and temperature have a notably distinct influence on the fundamental colour of the Siamese. Therefore young Siameses should be discouraged from lounging on radiators, and adult ones should not be fed on too much meat, if the white of their fur is not to darken.

Also established is that where white is dominant in the colour of the coat, a definite relationship exists between the pigmentation of the mucous membrane, the white of the hair, and deafness. This is the common case of albinism. Where the black pigment is dominant, the coat takes on that colour of brilliant soot which makes a black cat stand out among a group of grey or striped ones.

But, it must be admitted, the principles of this pigmentary distribution are not yet established: which is why the creating or controlled reproduction of such or such a coat too often remains in the region of the unknown.

To seize the occasion of a spontaneous mutation, to try to preserve it if it has an aesthetic or practical interest, still remains the chief object of breeding.

Felinotechnics misses no opportunity to achieve this aim, and has often succeeded. But nothing would have come of these successes if the societies of breeders or fanciers of high-bred cats had not had the initiative to establish standards, that is to say, to get together and codify the lines, colouring and measurements of the various breeds.

Every breeder has to strive to achieve and maintain the characteristics of these standards, by following the points of evaluation embodied in each of these definite details, and by rejecting any individual that does not correspond to the official type.

In this way the standards of our acknowledged breeds, such as Siamese, Persian, Chartreux, Burman, Abyssinian, etc., will be made definitive, while we look forward to new varieties and breeds in the future.

9. SIAMESES

Show judges officially allot the following scale of points to pure-bred Siameses:

Form and shape:

Head	.	.	.	.	15 points
Ears	.	.	.	.	5 ,,
Eyes	.	.	.	.	5 ,,
Body	.	.	.	.	15 ,,
Paws and Feet	.	.	.	5 ,,
Tail	.	.	.	.	5 ,,

50 points

Colour:

Eyes	.	.	.	.	15 points
Markings	.	.	.	.	10 ,,
Body	.	.	.	.	10 ,,
Hair texture	.	.	.	.	10 ,,
General condition	.	.	5 ,,

50 points

However, it is not strictly and solely by these figures that their value and fidelity to 'type' can be judged, but as much on the psychological as on the physical level.

'It is difficult to imagine', wrote Jean Cocteau for *Chat Beauté*, 'the tricks that a Siamese can invent to make an inert object as alive, terrible and cunning as himself. It makes one believe that cats share the particularities of human life, when they play a game of pretences, a strange game consisting of approaching a moving object and cornering it, and endowing it with life if it is motionless . . .'

More than any other breed, Siameses have this gift of dramatizing a private play, of acting out their own game; and – whether it is a mad gallop in pursuit of a cork or desolated wailings in front of a closed door – they 'play up' as the happiest cats in the world if only one admires them, or as the saddest if one gives them a bit of sympathy.

Coming into the world clothed immaculately in pure white, the little Siameses adapt themselves, as it were, gradually to life's hypocrisies. Growing up, they put a sombre mask across their beautiful, sky-coloured eyes; they glove and shoe themselves with dark suede; and they grow old enveloped more and more in their twilight-coloured dress, like philosophic old mandarins to whom human antics are of little interest.

LONG AND SHORT TAILS

Certainly men can say or write absurdities when they get involved in empirical zootechnics, when they presume to establish canons of pure beauty and to interfere with the creatures' reproduction to such ends as they deem appropriate or because some anatomical detail suits their whim or their interest.

Thus, in regard to Siamese cats, there is the dispute about long-tailed and short-tailed ones, which has lasted for twenty years. Because certain kittens are born (quite frequently, it is true) with the caudal appendage more or less stumpy, knotted or cut short so as to be no more than a bun or twisted cord, some breeders maintain in all seriousness that these anomalies are the attributes of the great, the pure, the only Siameses of distinction.

More sensibly, English breeders, whose acquaintance with

the Siamese dates back almost seventy years, have always noted in their official standard that Siameses should have a long, pointed tail, and have merely tolerated at the worst a hook at the end.

You may think this is just aesthetic cavilling. But the error which the French committed had rather unexpected repercussions on breeding.

Instead of perfecting each of the two varieties, long-tailed and short-tailed, it was attempted, in order to satisfy everyone, to cross the two types. The result was lamentable. Pure Siameses disappeared, and too many dark-masked, dark-gloved cats shown or sold today under this appellation are only distantly related to the true Siameses.

What, then, are the characteristics of these cats? The very first specimens introduced into Europe were brought to London in 1884 by Mrs Veley, sister of the British Consul at Bangkok; the first ones in Paris, much later, belonged to M Auguste Pavie, a Frenchman long resident in Siam who had presented them to the menageries of the old Botanic Gardens.

If the description of them given at that epoch can be believed, the royal cat of the Siamese court was a large cat with oblong skull, muscled loins, very steady blue eyes, and a long tail. Altogether the Siamese type of distinction rather resembles that little hieratical god found in the museum at Cairo and more reminiscent of the long-lined cheetah than of the thick-set, chubby-cheeked tiger or lion.

The long head, with its wide-set eyes, thins progressively in a straight line to the muzzle: so says, in short, the standard of the Siamese Club of England, which wields the power of law.

The ears, rather close together, solid at the base, must be large and pointed.

The body is of medium girth, lithe, long, with relatively thin paws and taller in front; the feet should be small and never round, the tail long and slender.

The colour? The colour of distinction is 'seal pointed', a clear coat with extremities of 'seal brown', but the colour fashionable tomorrow may be what you will, for breeders, like gardeners, have something of the creative eternally unsatisfied nature of artists. To create something that departs from nature's archetypal pattern, like the legendary blue rose or new Siameses of exceptional shades, would be exciting indeed.

Rostand maintained that the Siamese, born white as it is, would remain so if brought up in a warm room. The experiment might be worth trying some day.

The Blue Pointed is a Siamese similar to the others, with eyes of a Mediterranean blue, but masked, gloved and crowned with bluish-grey.

The Chocolate Pointed differs from those mentioned above only in his extremities, in his case milk-chocolate coloured; though the standard does not specify the proportions of chocolate and milk to be corresponded to in this definitive type.

All these three Siamese types (Seal, Blue and Chocolate) have one Asiatic characteristic in common: Oriental eyes, which must be a little slanted but never squinting.

Then there is a new variety to be cited: a cat which is all the rage because of its rarity: the Siamese with an orange mask, the Gold Pointed.

Gloved and crowned with orange, and with a straight tail, of course, this cat is not yet officially recognized. Will it have the long blue eyes of its breed or, coming down a peg or two, will its creators merely prescribe that its eyes are to be round and green or yellow? Why not? At all events, genetics would be well advised to remember the atavistic throwbacks, that hinder more often than they help scientific aims.

In the midst of all this fuss, what is to become of the true Siamese cat? The example of the American cat should suffice to show that there are limits which ought not to be gone beyond.

The Burmese cat is in fact a Siamese with eyes that are yellow and even, alas, round. Fortunately it is very rare, but boosted by the fashion, it apparently fetches fabulous prices. Rare, why? If the breed is a definitive one, it should be quite as prolific as other breeds of cats; and if it differs in a certain respect from the so-called 'Siamese' cats, why cross it with these, to the detriment of the blue, chocolate or orange Siameses already so controversial?

Only Marcel Chamonin seems to be uneasy about this, and according to him it is only by a thorough-going return to the true Siamese strain that we can hope to avert the disappearance of a distinguished breed so jealously preserved, until this day, by the Far East.

WHERE ARE THE SIAMESES OF YESTERYEAR?

At the whim, as he is, of fanciers who are more intent on achieving novelties than on looking after the Siamese, will this cat, to whom royal origin is attributed but who is now mismatched solely to make him rare and expensive, be able to keep his individuality?

If it was only that the texture of the hair or the colour of the eyes was to be varied, that would not matter: it is necessary to satisfy the reigning fashions. But it is not a question of superficial differences in the coat; but one of profound mis-alliances, of more radical cross-breeding that often manifests itself in serious imbalance, both externally and internally.

Blind fashion has made the affectionate, playful, patient, mischievous, bright Siameses of the past into inarticulate cats with discoloured grey eyes, often globular heads, heavy stomachs and stout limbs, with timorous, quarrelsome, touchy or apathetic characters, frequently jealous and aggressive.

How and why? There is no scientific law as yet to explain all this; but where the strain is pure and the type definitive, where confidence and calmness have been gradually established over a period of generations, the animal's character is at peace. But where different strains, various influences and contradictory tendencies meet and clash, there are insecurity, disturbances, the play of blind forces and instincts, and altogether the triumph of malady.

10. BLUE CATS

I am well aware that it is heretical to speak of 'blue cats' – apart from blue Persians – rather than of 'Chartreux' and 'Russian Blues' (otherwise even known as 'American cats' or 'Maltese cats').

I know too that the British Blue is only a democratic snob that one could not confuse with the two above-mentioned.

But how can we avoid confusion between cats of the same colour and, to a certain extent, of the same type of hair, unless we give some general information about the Blues, before going into detail about each type?

Only twenty-five years ago Dr Jumaud, in his inaugural lecture before the Faculty of Medicine of Lyons, gave the names of American cat and Maltese cat to the Chartreux cat (*catus Carthusianorum*):

'They are also found in Russia,' he said, 'where they form the sub-breeds of Morossan and Caucasian.'

So the confusion was extreme, even among the greatest specialists of the time. Today, Blues are distinctly classified, although their description and the scale of points of each is based on the classic Chartreux, properly so-called.

Where does he come from? From the alley-cat: since by the admission of the English themselves, the British Blue is a blue cat of 'European' extraction.

This is the grey-blue cat, rather light, short-haired, with great yellow or orange eyes and a well-proportioned body, neither too stout nor too thin, that appears from time to time in a litter, come from some mysterious shore of the chromosomic ocean.

Is the type so clearly defined as to make us certain of admitting a definitive breed in him? By no means; for the light tabby markings, the more or less deep shades in the range of the blue itself, are common enough for the cautious standard to regard them as undesirable.

The scale of points is, however, well balanced: 50 points for the standard common to all Europeans, 25 points for the hair colour, and 25 also for the colour of the eyes, which must never be green and so turn the British Blue into a Russian Blue cat.

THE RUSSIAN BLUE

The range here is even more eclectic and flexible: all the colourings from pearl grey to glossy grey-blue are allowed in judging the breed.

The Russian cat (which has nothing in common with the so-called 'Tobolskan' cat with its medium-long, reddish hair) comes even closer to the slim, muscled, graceful proportions of the long-lined cat of the Pharaohs. His prescribed features are: narrow skull, receding forehead, head describing a triangle, long slender ears, and a green Asiatic gaze like that of the mummified cats with their enamelled eyes.

In the comparison of the Chartreux Blue with the Russian Blue, the boundary-line between the two classic types, within the same colour, has for once been clearly and sensibly defined.

In the Russian Blue, long legs, a short, glossy coat, and – what the standard does not specify – almost straight shoulders and a narrow chest.

In the Chartreux, a squat neck, round head with small ears and full face, with eyes of a steely yellow-orange, generous chest, limbs relatively short and well-muscled; altogether heavy, massive, with a slightly woolly fleece.

The Chartreux is a peasant, the Russian Blue an aristocrat.

It is fortunate that these two cats are able to be differentiated physically, since on the emotional plane there are no great differences between our stout worthy of a Chartreux (whom Dr Jumaud called 'lazy and indolent') and the Russian cat, who is intrinsically marked with the Slavic character.

During the very brief Russian summer, our colleague has said, the blue cats used to wander at large in the woods, and then in the winter they would be confined in the snow-covered *isba*, with nothing to do but eat and sleep.

Doubtless it is to this enforced hibernation that the erstwhile Russian Blues and today's Chartreux owe their thick, soft, close hair, soft as otter-fur, which industry – alas! – has begun to exploit.

11. PERSIANS AND
BURMANS

Will Persians, who before the war were called 'angoras', dethrone the Siamese, who are being made 'commoner' by their low commercial value?

For anyone who has bred or observed both of these breeds, the question is a meaningless one, as there are so many differences between these two types of the feline kind.

The Persian is as far removed from the Siamese as Sancho Panza was from Don Quixote.

To begin with, let us put an end, as Dr E. Dechambre urges, to this expression 'angora', which is current only among the uninitiated to designate the cat with long fur.

The characteristic of 'long, silken hair', having in all probability appeared one day as an hereditary mutation in the history of cats, is not an attribute exclusive to the species. There are angora rabbits, angora guinea-pigs and angora dogs, from the Yorkshire terrier to the Afghan hound. There are even goats of this kind, and doubtless it is to the fact that these goats exist in Angora that we owe the application of the term to Persian cats (which keep this other usurped name too, for all that they no longer come from Persia).

The Persian was imported from Italy in 1551 by Pietro del Lavale. One hundred years later Ménard smuggled the first long-haired cat across the French frontier.

Today the Persian is 'made in England' and, zootechnically speaking, we have to bow to this new success.

More important than the considerable returns from Persian cats on the international market, the perfecting of this little English masterpiece indicates the excellence to which the breeding of pedigree cats has attained.

Proportioned like a horse, with his large, short paws, superb plume of a tail, which he sometimes carries stiff as a taper, his big, globular head crowned by little rounded ears, and his large face illuminated by the most beautiful eyes in the world, the Persian cat is an aristocrat.

Contemplative? Indolent? Not a bit of it. Under his nonchalant, satiated air, this pretended unconcern masks the same latent anxiety, the same nervousness that all cats have inherited from their ancestors.

When he is suddenly roused by fear, his eyes on fire and his claws brandished, the black Persian is a veritable dragon, far more terrifying than the rowdiest alley-tom.

In their normal state, however, Persians are the gentlest, most well-behaved, most contented cats in the world.

Physically there is no type more tough at the adult stage. Swathed in their beautiful coat, they are rarely troubled by the cold. In summer, stretched out in the sun, abandoned to an Oriental lassitude, they seem to live at a slower pace; and perhaps this is why they survive illness and infection better than any other breed.

A dozen varieties make up the breed: white, black, cream-coloured, tortoise-shell, smoked, tabby, chinchilla. To be thorough we must add to these classic colourings white Persians with orange eyes and white Persians with blue eyes. It is a fact that the cats very aptly ranked under this term constitute nine-tenths of the long-hairs, since (apart from the Kmer, a very controversial type) the Burman is the only long-haired representative of other cats.

Distinguishing features of Persians? Defects to be avoided? The scale of points used in judging each of these different varieties? There are enough manuals devoted to these details for me to feel that I can refer any reader wanting to get all the available information to those works or to specialist clubs.

BURMANS

Let us rather discuss the Burman cat, since he is alone in this category. The Burman cat, who at the moment ends the list of long-hairs, establishes the link between Persians and Siamese. From the former he gets his convex forehead, thick whiskers, luxuriant fur, bushy tail, grand manner. From the latter he derives his elongated head, his steadier blue eyes and his coat of a creamy white, with ears, tail and paws of dark brown, but the extremities of these dipped in flawless white.

However, the Burman is neither a Siamese nor a Persian. He is the sacred cat of Burmese legend, that has so appealed to the imagination of man. A legend that is constantly growing, even embroidered by poets, but the essence of which was told to me long before the war, in 1926 if memory serves me rightly, by Mme Marcelle Adam, then President of the Central Feline Society, who was the first person in Paris to be acquainted with this beautiful, extremely rare cat from the mountains of Lugh.

'It was in the time when Mun-Ha, the old Kittah priest, with his beard of gold that the god Song-Hio himself had plaited, dwelt in contemplation of Tsun Kyan Kse, the sapphire-eyed goddess who presides over the transmutation of souls.

'For oracle he had a white cat, his cat Sinh. This latter, unmoving, also lived to contemplate the goddess, with all the transparent depth of his gold-flecked gaze.

'One evening, at moonrise, the accursed Siamese barbarians having advanced on the precincts, Mun-Ha appealed to the fates that were threatening his religion, and slipped away into death, laden with years and with anguish.

'It was then that the miracle, a miracle of sudden transmutation, took place. Sinh, the cat, leapt on to the sacred throne, leant against his old master's silvery head, and the white hairs of his back instantly turned gold-coloured in the flash of gold which the statue of the goddess irradiated.

'And his yellow eyes, that had been the yellow of Tsun Kyan Kse's gold, suddenly turned blue, the deep sapphire-blue of the eyes of the goddess; and his paws and ears took on the dark colour of the ground – except for his toes, which, clutching the venerable skull of his master, remained white.

'And the look which he slowly turned on the priests was so imperious, dominating, powerful, that the quelled Kittahs obeyed him, closed the temple gates, and going through the underground rooms repelled the invader.

'Sinh, the cat of the miracle, died seven days later, following the death of Mun-Ha, and taking with him the high priest's too-perfect spirit.

'Seven more days passed, and as the assembled Kittahs were wavering as to which of them should have the power to choose a successor to the high priest, they saw the hundred cats of the temple approaching slowly – all with white coats reflecting the gold, and eyes that had the sapphire-blue of the goddess. The entire hundred, white-gloved, made a ring round Ligoa, the youngest of the priests.

'Since then, whenever a sacred cat dies at the temple of Lao-Tsun, the soul of a Kittah priest accompanies it to the paradise of Song-Hio.'

'Woe to anyone who even unwittingly', the legend also says, 'puts an end to one of these worshipped cats. The worst punishments will be in store for him, without his guilty, tortured soul ever finding any rest for the whole of eternity.'

One wonders how Mr Vanderbilt managed to acquire a couple of these vigilantly guarded cats just after the First World War, and how others – none of whom were struck dead – were able to achieve so large a posterity for the breed. We have had champion Burmans by the dozens, leading up to those successful intermarriages with the gloved Siamese, so starting the dynasty of 'Arakans', 'Rangoons', 'Mandalayans'.

There is a good deal of mystery here, but then mystery and legend are an essential part of the cult.

12. OTHER BREEDS, OTHER LEGENDS

Travellers tell fine tales. Special cats are reported to be found in Gambia, Turkey, Bengal, at the Cape of Good Hope, awaiting the pleasure of the discoverer. It is the same with cat-heraldry as with our human patents of nobility: someone has to found the dynasty.

The cat's genealogy is of very recent date, and we must not expect too much from it.

MANX CATS

No one can maintain that the Manx cat, the tail-less cat, actually originated on that pleasant island between Dublin and Liverpool. If the English did not seem to have a marked weakness for so-called 'anourous' animals (from the Bobtail to the Welsh Corgi) we might be tempted too, as many authors have been, to fix the origin of these cats in the Malayan archipelago, where apparently long-tailed cats are rare.

However that may be, the 'Rumpie' of the Isle of Man is known today throughout the world, with his back paws a little higher than the front ones, his curious, jerky gait like that of an anxious hare, and that double fur like a rabbit's with longer hair on the surface and softer hair at the base.

What is the why and wherefore of his strange deprivation that in fact constitutes his charm? The experts do not go into this. They say: 'The breed is naturally anourous'; that is to say, congenitally deprived of the final coccygeal vertebra and any caudal vertebrae that could act as skeleton for the least embryo of a tail.

Other creatures are born thus in Scotland, and out of good sense or indifference, the Manxmen themselves do not trouble their heads about the matter. There is an explanation, as a matter of fact: that at the time of the Flood and the launching of the Ark, this cat was the last to step on board, just as Noah was shutting the door, which, through having cut off the cat's tail, gave the name *coupée* in French to the entering-port of a ship.

Then there is that other scientific fantasy according to which the Manx cat is descended from an astounding match between a female cat and a rabbit.

The export demand for these cats having trebled and quadrupled before the war, the people of the Isle of Man were disturbed to realize one day that the breed was regressing. The litters were becoming rarer; and in such or such a line the third generation of young would be rickety, and the fourth, 80 per cent of the time, born dead.

A rival then came to the fore: an absurd 'Stumpy' which, with all the qualities of a real Manx cat, had – as yet imperceptible, but there beyond a doubt – the pretentious tip of a tail.

The breeders got together, forming an association at once. This defence syndicate took up arms, and since then all the shows and national markets have displayed genuine, self-respecting Manxes – black, white, grey, striped, streaked or tabby, with the tail as it should be (that is, completely non-existent).

HAIRLESS CATS

It is true that completely naked cats also exist: cats without fur, among which we have succeeded in determining a strange

127

mutation linked to a recessive gene.

Did the race of hairless cats actually exist in Mexico? Did it originate from the short-haired cats of Paraguay? This is not beyond the realms of possibility, as these hairless cats are not initially bare; they do not come into the world so, as Andre Sécat has pointed out. Initially they have a covering of down, which falls out after the first week. Afterwards there is another growth of down, which lasts for two months: time for the kittens to be weaned and sufficiently developed to survive. In its turn, this thin coat falls out during the next few weeks.

When the cats have attained the age of six months, they are then, but then only, hairless cats, perfectly smooth-skinned. Are they beautiful? That is a different matter. But should you be tempted to possess one, it would be useless to look for it on the market. There are no hairless cats professionally bred. They are simply a curiosity of creation.

THE SO-CALLED ABYSSINIAN CATS

Up to now 'hairless' cats have attracted no one.

But now we come to something new in France: the so-called Abyssinian cat which actually comes from England.

Why this name? The Abyssinian Embassy is able to shed no light on the matter. There are no Abyssinian cats on the shores of the Negus. But this is of no consequence. The breed so-called has so many qualities, so much beauty, such gentleness and charm, that it represents, in my humble opinion, the perfect cat.

What is the Abyssinian cat like? He is the prototype of cat.

Imagine on a smaller scale the universally known cat whose statue in the Louvre has so often been reproduced in pictures, or terra cotta, bronze or plaster sculptures: this great hieratical cat, seated on his hindquarters, with his front legs very straight, his reptilian head, his long pointed ears, and his body at once supple, elegant and solid.

Cover him in a coat borrowed from the red-brown field-hare, with each hair of a reddish-brown dotted with black or brown.

Add the dignified bearing of the most beautiful Siamese, the melting gaze (yellow or green) of a characteristic alley-cat, and the keen intelligence of a well-bred Persian kitten.

And then you have the Abyssinian.

A cat such as every household would want to own, if only the present-day breeders could succeed in producing them in large numbers, at reasonable prices.

'No lines, no stripes, no marks,' says the standard, which very rightly requires that the inner parts of the paws and the stomach should be of a shade harmonizing with the principal colour (the preference being for orange-brown): 'no marks or streaks.'

A well-proportioned cat, as perfect as if he had come to life from some hypogea.

I have seen the Abyssinian cat on all the subterranean frescoes of the Valley of Kings. I have seen him again at Medinet-Habou, sculpted on the columns of the principal entrance to the temple. I have seen him at the Cairo Museum, and again in some anonymous silhouette appearing on the faded wall of a mud-hut by the Nile, or in 'Chinese shadows'. I have seen him splashing wantonly in the muddy canals by the fields of fenugreek near the Colossi of Memnon. He must remember how he used to hunt in the marshes, or lie in wait, in the tip of a papyrus bark, for the wild geese.

He is the animated phantom of the cats of the Pharaohs; and his name, taken from a country where he is quite unknown, is sheer fantasy. The very coat that he has adopted for his reincarnation is not a cat's coat: he has a rabbit's fur. As a matter of fact, he is sometimes called 'Cunny' or 'cat-bunny'.

The English describe him as 'ticked' or 'flecked'; and this chief characteristic also taking the genus-name 'agouti'[1] (and being rather prevalent among other wild animals) might well denote a return to what we like to regard as the true cat of our ancestors, the original of the domestic cat.

---

[1] The agouti is a hare-like animal of the West Indies

What if the Abyssinian did come to England straight from Africa in 1868? Or what if he is really the offspring of a female cat of Kaffraria and a common alley-tom? What if this fact was established by Mr Brooke in 1920? Whether this new-comer in the feline firmament is the result of chance or of exceptional selection is of little importance.

What is significant is that this cat revives forgotten characteristics, a combination of felicitous points that make of him, genuinely or accidentally, a kind of masterpiece.

We do know that it is impossible to predict, without the definite approval of experts as sincere as they are knowledge-able, if a male and female *apparently* belonging to this breed will definitely produce Abyssinian offspring.

We know that, though this beautiful 'rediscovered' cat is extremely delicate, he could become one of the hardiest cats tomorrow. If only the breeders can resist the desire to breed him carelessly, just to meet the immediate demand, and so injuring the breed in commercializing it at short notice.

The Abyssinian, contrary to the Siamese, does not seem to be very prolific. He is a big raw meat eater; and he is in better form at a temperature with little variation (61° to 65°) than freely exposed to the caprices of the weather.

For this cat, surprisingly enough, not the least 'back-ground' of legend has been dug up. At the moment this is not an essential, but it will become one.

The Abyssinian would have had his legend by now if only historians could come to an agreement as to the exact epoch of the cat's arrival in Ancient Egypt. Ruppel declares the first cats of the Pharaohs to have been those brought from Ethiopia, with the consent of the Abyssinians, by Ousirtasen I. How-ever, this conquering prince belonged to the Twelfth Dynasty, and the cat was already described in Egypt in the Fifth.

However it may be, if cats are to be saved thanks to selec-tion, to the evaluation of certain breeds, to breeding; if of the two ills we must choose the lesser; if there is to succeed – to the wretched, hunted, starved, misunderstood, unjustly mal-treated cats who no longer have even the gutter, but only palings and squares – an elite of cats jealously chosen, drawn from a very few exemplars, I believe that one can safely make the following prediction:

The Abyssinian cat, revenant as he is, will also be the great cat of the future.

13. A PLEA FOR CATS

To think that there was a time when an entire household would don mourning for a cat's death, when those who loved him would shave their eyebrows as a sign of profound distress, when the priests would embalm his corpse in a special necropolis and carry it amidst great pomp to private cemeteries, of which the most famous was that of Bubastis, near the temple of the goddes Bast.

The adored cats' mummies would then be laid to rest in stone sarcophagi; statues of bronze or gilded wood (and we know how rare wood is in Egypt) perpetuated their memory and preserved the mystery of vanished splendours in their enamelled eyes.

Were they of a definitive breed, jealously selected, these extinct cats of Ancient Egypt, or were they the offspring of chance matches? No one can be certain.

Mingled since then at random in their fights, meetings and loves, at the whim of their pleasures and misfortunes, cats are victimized by a host of unfavourable prejudices, as violent as that passionate adoration which formerly centred on them.

All too many people dislike cats not for any reason but as a matter of principle. All too many people dislike them who have never so much as stroked one with the tips of their fingers.

How can you say, my dear lady, that you have a horror of them, if you have never been scratched, bitten, or disappointed by one in any way whatsoever. Without any of these valid reasons, your aversion must be prejudice – or a phobia.

The word shocks you? Nevertheless ...

I understand: 'When you were a little girl, you were playing with the family cat one day ...' But, with some reason, a cat, even the family one, is not and does not want to be a toy. You might recall what patience he must have needed to submit to 'playing' with you, as you put it. In turn, you used to wash him, dress him up in rags, harness him to a shoe-box, and roll him in a napkin. Not to speak of the whiskers that were cut, the bows tied to his tail, and the thousand and one other pranks, all the thoughtless tyranny that childhood could impose on him.

Between ourselves, do you really believe he was in the wrong that day when he warned you, with a swipe of his exasperated claws, that you were going too far?

You may point out that cats do not scratch only children. It is true they also scratch clumsy people and fools.

But the fact is that the cat does not need to ponder or weigh things up for any length of time, in order to express himself. He is neither cruel nor wicked. He simply knows how to make himself respected. He stays on the defensive. You never see a cat bite or scratch out of stupid cruelty.

'Every man for himself' is his motto. It is not necessarily a wicked one, still less one denoting selfishness.

The cat's selfishness? I do not believe in it. Two cats never fight, except over a question of love, once they are assured of the vital minimum of food. They even go in for exchanging courtesies over their dishes. And they provide many examples of generosity, self-abnegation and a courageous social sense.

There are cases like that of the female cat who, grievously bitten by a big dog, resisted him to her last breath, so as to protect her two terrorized kittens. Or that other who, to prevent an eagle carrying off a kitten, fastened on to his side; until the bird of prey, crushing her, took flight, dragging her with him. The duel continued for five hundred yards and ended in the dizzy fall of two corpses.

It is no fairer to say that the cat is wicked. To be sure, there are the occasional unbalanced, even sadistic, ones to be met with; but why should there not be aggressive lunatics and invalids among cats, as among all higher beings? I know a striped cat, belonging to an old bachelor friend of mine, who cannot resist the imperceptible grating of a silk stocking on a woman's calf under the table. This slight noise, almost inaudible to us, throws him into a fit of hypernervosity; just as irresistibly as the creaking of a door or the rubbing of two velvet stuffs together can exacerbate a woman's nerves. However, this kind of thing is the exception, and does not give us the right to infer the general from the particular.

One might even declare that there are fewer ill-natured cats than there are cruel dogs in the pathological sense, because there is less consanguinity among cats, consequently less danger of degeneration.

Is it that hereditary obedience to instinct alone which gives the cat his personality? Perhaps so. At all events, no other animal has a character that is more engaging, more marked, or more disquieting.

The cat eats when he is hungry, drinks when thirsty; and it is solely to satisfy his appetites that he brings himself out of his natural indolence.

But it is up to the dog to adjust to man's selfishness, to confirm his own slavery, to watch his master's eyes for the alms of a look. The cat offers no such submission, and that is what constitutes his charm.

You, sir, go on about disliking cats; you have swallowed all the current, unproven prejudices; that a black cat brings bad luck, that a yellow one is a hypocrite, a grey one lazy, a striped one a thief.

The fact is that cat-haters are afraid of seeing humanity reflected in the cat's behaviour. It is there, all right, complete as in a looking-glass, a false, distorting glass showing only our image.

The cruelty of cats is unconscious, while man inflicts suffering and death every day in cold blood.

Cats are accused of being sadistic; because their loves are violent. But have our human pleasures of the kind which, lightly (as Colette said), we call physical, a different reality?

The hypocrisy of cats? This is more than anthropological slander; it is calumny, current just because our judgement too often requires forced demonstrations. But the cat is utterly sincere. 'In cats', said Louis Pergaud, who was well acquainted with the species, 'a straightening of the eyebrows, a laying back of the ears, the bristling of the whiskers, or puckering of the nose, an imperceptible wrinkling of the lip, the extending or contraction of the eyelids, the lashing of the tail, and certain ways of hunching up and putting their weight on one paw, are precursory signs of the storm, and scarcely ever mislead one.'

How better could they warn one? They could hardly use words more eloquently to express their anger.

A hypocrite is someone who smiles, flatters and detests you, protesting his friendship the better to betray you afterwards. Perhaps you may prefer, to the cat's way, the crafty air with which certain watch-dogs will approach you on the sly and seize hold of your coat-tails if you make the least move away.

When the cat explodes in a fury, there is thunder and lightning at once, the light of murder in his eyes; and it is impossible to suppress or calm the storm which one's obstinacy or clumsiness in trying to abate it will often aggravate.

Surely this is anything but hypocritical. It is a faithful, accurate explanation of the explosive behaviour of an animal who is incapable of hiding his feelings, and who can never be brought to suppress them.

Are cats lazy? Well, good luck to them, if they are. Which one of us has not entertained the dream of doing just as he likes, when and how he likes, and as he likes?

The cat's greediness? In the name of what asceticism, what humility, should he be deprived of the choice of what he likes?

Is he a thief? Possibly. More exactly, a kleptomaniac. So many hundreds of thousands of cats have died of hunger that the instinct of making sure of the little extra still haunts and motivates many of them today who have all they need.

No, the cat is neither cruel, nor selfish, nor sadistic, nor hypocritical.

He is quite simply the cat, a creature whom no civilization has been able to reduce to slavery. It is too soon. The dog has been close to man for almost a million years. The cat is scarcely a contemporary of civilized man. The dog was the first animal to be enslaved, the cat the last to be domesticated.

Why should he have devoted himself, in a few tens of centuries, to man, who, except in Egypt, has never taken the trouble to observe him so as to understand him?

The cat is an independent being: it is this that irritates some people.

'With the qualities that we require of servants,' said Marivaux, 'what master would be capable of being an honourable valet?'

With the qualities of cleanliness, discretion, affection, patience, dignity and courage that cats have, how many of us, I ask you, would be capable of being cats?

Have I convinced you, sir? And you, madam, have I reassured you? I hope so. Now it only remains for you to choose between black or beige or white Persian, cream-coloured Siamese, speckled Abyssinian, or Russian Blue, or even one of the numerous 'European' cats, very much our own.

You will adopt him straight away, and if you do not get to the bottom of his mystery, at least your affectionate interest will preclude his martyrdom.

Which, all in all, promises you some of those hundred feline joys: the satisfied purr to soothe an idle hour, the caress which is returned like an echo to the fingers themselves, the irresistible grace of astonishing kittens – all these delightful, engaging things, to make you regret your past errors, triumph over your ignorance, and laugh at your discarded phobia.

Owning a Cat

As the reader may surmise, the foregoing pages have not been composed straight off.

This sort of documentation represents years of observation, research, experiments and reading of all kinds, from literary passages that may appear commonplace to the most guarded scientific information of the day.

Is this self-evident? I cannot judge. No book is indispensable, save that which you take up by chance one day just so as to verify, with scorn, that no one after you has dared to write on the subject.

Down through civilization and centuries, the cat has not failed to inspire poets, to intrigue physiologists and to interest psychologists profoundly; but the results of these works, the conclusions of these surveys, are all scattered in various publications as far removed one from the others on the library shelves as the Railway Directory, a translation of the Book of Hours of Sosostris, and the practical Vademecum of amateur bee-keepers.

Who will read this book? Cat-lovers? I hope so; and they, surely, will appreciate my attempt to collect all that can be gleaned, all that we think we know and have learned about their favourite companion. For them, the story might rest there.

But there are the indifferent, uninformed people: those who in the preceding pages may perhaps, as it were, have discovered the cat. The familiar pages that are going to follow are for them.

To the initiated, this last chapter will teach nothing that they do not know, but may be useful to the uninformed person who is anxious or curious to learn what to do and what not to do so as to live in perfect harmony with cats.

14. FROM PSYCHOLOGY TO COMFORT

We ll, it wasn't so difficult, after all.

Black as pitch as he is, with a funny white mark on his chin, or perhaps a grey or fawn background, streaked, striped or ringed, perhaps again rigged out all in white or brown-masked like the self-respecting Siamese that he is, or else a woolly Chartreux, a silky Persian or high-bred Abyssinian. You have a cat in the house.

Female or male?

What, you don't know?

You must learn how to tell a female from a male, even with new-born kittens. Don't laugh: the breeders themselves are sometimes at a loss over this when the cats are only a few days old.

Simply lift up the tail. You see two orifices. If they are almost juxtaposed, it is a female. If a definite space separates them, it is a male.

You would have preferred. . . . No, better not have any regrets. Tom or queen, both have their drawbacks, both their advantages; and, as the day may well come when you acquire a female to keep your male company, or a male to appease the female, you can begin equally well with one or the other. Meanwhile, hold on to him (or her) whom chance has bestowed on you.

You have a cat in the house? Then by the same token you have a microphone, an untrimmed candle, a battery, a photographic and radar apparatus, an entire high-fidelity recording machine that observes, notes, stores and retains everything – odours, sounds and images – before forming an opinion.

Do not force the issue. Let the newcomer make contact with his surroundings. The whole future harmony of the arrangement can depend on his initial contact. Do not make up to him too much, or try to persuade him, with some absurd onomatopoeia, that the feline language really holds no secrets for you.

Do not miaow. Be satisfied with 'thinking cat'.

Imagine that you are in an unknown country. Tell yourself that everything around you is suspect and threatening, unusual and dangerous. So then, grant the newcomer the very natural indulgence that you would have for a very small, bewildered child. And this comprehensive patience is even more essential, you must know, with the hypersensitive being that a cat of several weeks or several months is. There is the lift, with its deep rumblings as it passes each floor; there is that gulf of a staircase, and that monster of a vacuum-cleaner. There is that man smelling of tobacco and appearing to draw a tank at each paw, and that woman who fusses, and those howling children. Not to mention the telephone bell, which suddenly goes through one at the very moment when, happily dug in under some piece of furniture, one had thought to relax at last.

Let him be. Caught between curiosity to inspect, sniff and know everything, and the terror of being incautious, he will end by calming down. He will get used to all the noises, all the comings and goings, all your cries and gestures; and little by little, generally in three or four days, provided that none of these investigations with his senses is attended by a painful or unpleasant experience, it is he, reassured, who will make approaches to you.

As it happens, man is the only being who can liberate animals from their natural complex: flight. The tendency to flight is the most imperious instinct in all frightened or wild animals. The cat shakes this off as soon as he is with another being of definitely superior force: he no longer feels the need to keep his distance. That is to say, a man having progressively diminished the remoteness, the distance between them, the cat will no longer react at the moment when that 'escaping distance' is infringed. It is by a patient, gradual approach like this that tamers gain the confidence of the most suspicious animals.

In the same way you have to free your new friend from his complex. How? By using the only two recourses that equally govern the behaviour of individuals and groups: bread and circuses. Give him enough to eat, and do not forget that play is a channelling of the aggressive, fighting instinct and the best common ground of understanding.

To be logical, I should discuss feeding first, but that is so important a chapter of animal life, and the life of the cat in particular, that I think it best to go straight on to discuss play and training, and leave the question of feeding for later.

PLAY

Like all predatory animals, the cat never takes any interest in an inanimate prey. The bit of paper or the ball placed in the centre of the room will not make him move an inch; but should the wind imperceptibly stir the paper, or should a sloping place or a collision make the ball roll, the cat will immediately leap into action.

It is life, or the appearance of life, that sets him going and takes him out of himself.

A cat playing with a live sparrow or a mouse will catch it, put it on the ground, and with a swipe of his paw immobilize it as soon as the bird or rodent makes a move to escape. But should the victim, through fear or cunning, remain motionless, the attention of its thoughtless tormentor will relax to such an extent that often the mouse will have time to escape into a hole, or the bird will be able to take flight before the booby has recovered from his surprise.

So then, give your cat a symbolic prey. If the ball of paper artlessly thrown on to his nose does not succeed in rousing him, attach a cork or a rabbit's foot to the end of a string, excite his curiosity, and when he has made the acquaintance of one or other of these toys, throw the ball under a piece of furniture, or attach the cork to a doorknob. He won't need you, after this.

EDUCATION

Freed from anxieties by play, and by meals from that other slavery which is hunger, the household cat will be in the best condition to submit to that indispensable discipline: education or training.

In the opinion of all animal teachers, training is, properly speaking, no more than disciplined play.

In the case of the cat it could never be a matter of inducing so independent a creature to do, say, acrobatics or rope-dancing tricks on demand.

Certain showmen, happily very few, exhibit trained cats, balancers, acrobats, cats who play ridiculous fancy-dress games with wedding-gowns or policemen's helmets. Often these showmen train the cats by means of privation, terror-ization, and suffering; but then the creatures are only robots in cat's skin: cats for whom revolt or escape is no longer a possibility, and who have been cornered into a choice of obedience or death. I have known only one performing cat who performed for love of his master: one only.

But I have seen music-hall cats who have had their claws extracted and two unfortunate cats pressed into service as artistes because they were blind.

Blind, a cat! What a misfortune! For the cat is one of those rare higher mammals whose eyes can look into the sun with

impunity and can capture the faintest light, the least percept-
ible reflection in the night.

No, no one can boast of 'possessing' a cat: Paul Morand,
writer, diplomat and cat-lover, who knew all about cats and
people, acknowledged that 'in all cases, a cat owns *you*.'

Experiments have proved that the cat is not so stubborn, as
determinedly limited as one tends to think. Some original
research, presented by Professor Tsaï at the International
Congress of Psychology at Montreal, showed that the cat is
not evidently so dominated by instinct that he cannot be
changed with a little application and patience.

A cat obliged to live on friendly terms with rats, and to help
them, in order, at the same time as they are fed, to get his own
meals, adapts himself in less than three months, and ends by
understanding, perforce or willingly.

Do you think that a cat who resists being shut up in a
basket when he knows that this means a visit to the vet, will
climb into it with the best will in the world if he knows that
the basket can also signify an outing to the country?

'I never trouble about whether the tigers I want to train
understand me,' says Gilbert Houcke, a remarkable animal-
fighter whose act is a free-for-all with nine wild beasts. 'I just
try to understand what my big cats are thinking, I try to guess
their reactions and feelings, and – surrender? hostility? indifference! – what I can expect from them.'

Subtlety, fine distinctions: all-important in our relations
with animals and especially with felines, be they tigers or
Siameses.

Never provoke a cat. Never try to get him to obey you with
shouts or blows. Never punish a cat unless you are certain
that he is guilty. Cats, like children, have a natural sense of
justice, and are ready to pay only if they are in the wrong.

With a bare minimum of training, a well-disposed cat will no longer be a menace to the cleanliness of one's hall or the safety of one's carpets and furniture.

General hygiene, to begin with: as necessity knows no law.

If you have not got a garden in which your cat can revert to his wild-animal instincts, where do you expect him to relieve himself, unless you have made some arrangement for him?

'Cats are clean,' you may say.

But let us be clear about all this. I knew an adorable and timid little Persian whose evident discretion in this matter was so admirable that her mysteriousness and secrecy became alarming.

'The Lord only knows how this new cat is so clean!' her mistress enthused for a whole week. 'She has been here a week now, and never done a thing.'

She was indeed very clean, this little cat with a disarming expression; but as the other three cats of the household forbade her access to the lavatory she had found somewhere else: one fine morning she was surprised in the kitchen, in appropriate position on the sink.

However, do not count on having one of those well-bred cats (I have met only two, in thirty years' experience of cats) who go to the w.c. and even pull the chain! One of them carried his discretion to the point of covering his tracks with newspaper. This kind of jewel is very rare. You had better do your cat the favour of giving him a place from the first. A tray, a flat, firm, solid tray made of iron or hide, large enough for him to be able to get on it conveniently, and not one of those jugglers' plates that would be enough to make him want to go elsewhere.

Sand? Crumpled paper? Ashes? Sawdust? Sand is perhaps the most sanitary; it clings to the paws less than ashes. Sawdust has the advantage that it can be burnt. Paper is economical. So it is up to you to decide.

At all events, whether it be a question of a dog or a cat, the principle in this kind of education remains the same: when, assisted by your patience and his necessity, you have obtained a result in the specified place, then and then only show your approval by a few short words spoken in an affectionate tone: 'Good! Good boy! Very good!'

On the other hand, do not hesitate to scold the offender on the spot, in the event of a mishap; to carry him off immediately to his tray, and there to caress him again. The dullest cat will very soon catch on that 'there' means punishment, displeasure and misunderstandings, and that 'here' means caresses. He will choose accordingly for the future.

One is ready to believe that all cats are clean because one sees how industriously the least little kitten will scrabble up imaginary earth on the floor. All cats perform this gesture, but as often in the sawdust of their tray or on the sand of the alley as on the kitchen floor. This is a remote instinct, now no longer useful or necessary, the purpose of which is to leave no trace for the enemy, and which no longer signifies the least consideration of hygiene in our cats.

So the cat's own instinct of cleanliness is not to be counted on too much.

BODILY HYGIENE

Because cats take care of their fur too, their hygiene has long been neglected. If every cat polishes and licks his hair, it is not out of vanity or cleanliness. They wash themselves, instinctively as well as necessarily, in order to combat deficiencies. In fact nature tirelessly renews the deposit of vitamin D on the surface of their coats: an indispensable factor accumulated the more the cat is exposed to the light. That is why cats know how to get the maximum benefit from ultra-violet rays (lunar or solar), and why nothing is worse than to interfere with his washing arrangements by bathing him too often. If one cleaned a cat's hair with some solvent or other just twice a day, the best-fed and toughest tom would not survive three weeks.

Remember, though, that the cat scrabbles in his tray, walks in the garden and sleeps on the garage roof; that he can harbour parasites, that his hair can get dirty, and that cats, long-haired ones especially, cannot comb or brush themselves as we do.

An old hair-brush, a steel comb, or else one of those little flexible curry-combs with metallic teeth set in india-rubber that are found in all shops that sell collars and leads, will do the job perfectly.

How often? Every morning, if this is not too much to ask. Your cat will be in transports, not for aesthetic reasons but because he enjoys as much as we do the sensation of well-being that comes from massage or friction with a rough glove.

In this way, all the vexation that his seasonal moulting can inflict on a well-kept house will be avoided.

In principle this moulting takes place from spring to summer. It is a natural phenomenon of the same order as the changing of coat in most mammals or the serpent's shedding of its skin. Thus it is better to expedite it than to try and retard or check it.

Except for the tail, you should get down to a real trim with the brush, and finish up with a rapid glossing of the fur with the help of a toilet glove lightly moistened in toilet vinegar.

For white-haired cats you should preferably use a dry shampoo (inert powder with a base of carbonate and talc) scented preferably with lavender or verbena, since these are the two perfumes that cats seem to find most tolerable – and once a week.

SHOULD CATS BE BATHED?

Why not? Although the cat, being a creature of the sun, is more susceptible than the dog to a sudden chill, it is very much in order to give a dirty, accidentally smelly cat a bath.

Cats who trust their masters readily accept this unwonted intervention and, in the event, lend themselves to it quite willingly. Short-haired cats, as we have seen, have not the holy terror of water that is popularly supposed. One August I met, between the islands of Lérins near Cannes, a black cat who was sailing in a little rubber boat with his young master, and who of his own accord would jump into the sea every quarter of an hour to fish and also, obviously, just for the fun of it.

However, bathing should be limited to the shortest possible time. Dry the coat first with a turkish towel, then with an electric dryer, finishing off with a vigorous brush. Not that cats catch cold easily (wild cats adapt themselves very well to snow; and in Haute-Marne before the war the Marquise de Scey Montbeliard used to own some Siameses who slept out when the temperature was 20° below freezing), but because they have not got that useful reflex of snorting, frisking about, keeping on the move, which the dog has, and because, if they are happily settled in life, they have a natural penchant for immobility.

Far from counting on stoves, radiators and other sources of heat to complete the drying process, on the contrary one does better occasionally to turn off these easy roasters that turn cats into kettles.

'Mummy,' a little girl said one day, 'listen to the cat boiling!' Deep as this purring is, that kind of sleep does them no good.

THE CLAWS

Jules Renard wrote in his *Journal*: 'A cat is the life and soul of furniture.'

Either the author of *Poil de Carotte* was speaking as a poet and had never kept a cat in his house, or else he had given up for lost whatever precious satins and handsome woods he had, not to speak of leather armchairs. Unless – and there is no other obvious explanation – he had taken the wise precaution of having their claws trimmed once a month.

For the cat's claws are extremely important in his life. What control he needs to keep these weapons back, so swift as they are to spring out of the fur, in order to force himself to make 'velvet paws'! If he occasionally forgets to keep them back and gets hold of a curtain or some clumsy person, he is scolded as though he has committed a crime. Now claws which are not exercised grow to the point of interfering with his walking. They break, fall out, become ingrown, just like human beings' nails.

The remedy is to cut them, if one is sufficiently sure of oneself not to make them bleed.

When? How? To what length? How often? Too short claws in a cat make him a cripple. Over-long ones make an invalid of him. Innumerable cats, gliding along a roof, have had a fatal fall because their masters thought it a good thing to cut these undesirable hooks to the quick.

The best thing is to let the creature take care of them himself. A plank of soft wood or a sheet of cork will generally serve the purpose very well. I prefer to these, however, an ingenious device first popularized in England and easy to construct oneself.

Get a small log of wood two or two and a half feet high and four to six inches in diameter. Stand it on end and fix it on two planks nailed together in the shape of a cross for support (as one does with Christmas trees to make them balance). Wrap this trunk in an old bit of carpet, preferably nailed inside out, that is, with the webbing outside; and you will have given your cat a most valuable pleasure: he will be able every morning to straighten himself against a tree-trunk, as it were, to stretch, dig in his claws and to scrape them two or three times on waking up, thus extending and flexing the muscles – as his ancestors did, and as all cats at large do.

The conclusion must not be too hastily drawn from this gesture that cats were tree-dwellers originally. Like all the mighty wild beasts (tigers, lions, etc.) who are capable only of either walking slowly or of moving in more or less rapid bounds, because they can neither run nor gallop, cats have the habit of clambering on to a piece of furniture or a rock, but always to a moderate height, just enough to enable them to drop on their enemy or their prey.

If they happen to climb higher, to a tree-top, they are at a loss as to getting down again.

Giddiness? Fear of space? These explanations are certainly

debatable, considering with what calm audacity a cat will move on the edge of a seven-storey roof, from what heights he can jump, with his supple resistance, and meet with no injury, where a dog would break all its bones.

15. FEEDING

The cat is an animal whom people don't bother about.

In Paris *la bouillie pour les chats* ('food for cats') means something that is a thoroughgoing mess.

People in the country take the attitude that cats 'shift for themselves', but these people don't complain any less loudly when a tom on the prowl steals a bit of meat from their kitchen.

How are cats expected to feed themselves without either hunting or stealing?

Your cat, whom you have singled out for the best of everything, will of course be nurtured and cosseted like a prince; but the road to hell is paved with good intentions, and if you want to spoil him, it is as well to know how to go about it.

Are you going to give him whatever pleases him, whatever he likes?

He likes chicken (with bones), small birds (with the feathers), fish (with bones). He enjoys liver, and in general all offal.

This is because every domestic cat harks back to his wild feline ancestry. After a tiger or lion has disembowelled its prey, it laps up a little blood and then immediately attacks the viscera. We know why this is: afraid of being surprised and not having time for the whole feast, they first devour the spleen or the blood-gorged liver, rich in life-giving vitamins – guided as they are by the same natural instinct which makes the delicate Pekingese hanker after the lean bones that are denied him.

In the matter of nutrition, the carnivores do have imperious needs, which it is indispensable to know.

They need to make a large-scale consumption of mineral salts, fats and nitrates, with which nature provides them in the wild state, but which are usually lacking in the unsuitable diet imposed by domestication.

As a result, they display tastes that are sometimes surprising but only superficially baffling. There are cats living in a half-wild state in the Cameroons, and commuting between the household and the jungle or forest, who have an unexpected taste for dry bread, chocolate or preserves, but disdain sausages and sardines.

Others prefer that standard daily fare that 150 different firms offer to the 48 million cats that America provides for and to the 6,600,000 English cats. And others, lastly, turn up their noses at this substantial stuff and prefer to be treated to some old herring.

Every taste is natural. Whether it corresponds likewise to good sense is another matter.

Animal instinct in regard to this is not as infallible as is popularly accepted. Avoid giving your pets, even if they have a fondness for these things, certain products like that questionable city-milk, or that spleen which happens to be decomposing, appearances to the contrary; and also put a ban on those bony scraps of bird or dangerous fish heads, which have exacted a terrible toll from innumerable greedy cats.

WHAT THE EXPERTS THINK ABOUT IT

What do the experts think about it? The nutritional chemists as well as the vets? First of all, that the cat is not a dog, and that the domestic cat is too much of a newcomer to be transformed, like the dog, into an omnivore.

The cat is not a dog, and the digestive apparatus of these two animals is not yet exactly interchangeable. The cat's small intestine measures about sixty-five inches, his colon fourteen inches, but his caecum is scarcely curved and not in the least spiral like that of the dog. In the dog, the two intestines are almost of the same diameter, while the cat's colon is very bulky in proportion to the small intestine. Finally, the cat's stomach is lined with a rich and effective mucous membrane, such that it alone accounts for three-quarters of the work (the food normally remains here for twelve hours).

The teeth are also less numerous (twenty-four in the young cat and thirty in the adult), with very small incisors and long, sharp and pointed canines: a set of teeth made for tearing and wrenching. What little chewing the cat does is motivated solely by caution, since his pharynx is narrow and his mucous membrane very sensitive.

Hitherto even cat-lovers have fed their pets rather haphazardly. It is therefore a very good thing that skilled research is being undertaken today in England, Germany, America and Brazil, to arrive at the exact nutritional needs of the cat-world.

Already the norms of requirement are different according to whether the subject is a kitten or an adult, a female or a male.

I have before me the works of Dr Pottinger of Monrovia, California, of Mostyn, Morris, Irwin, Taylor and many others. All these surveys include regular samplings of the blood, daily weighings, chemical analyses, tables of metabolic rates, calorie charts, and all the precise methods and proofs that the most painstaking dieticians can dream up.

I shall spare the reader the details of these extremely masterly techniques. But their conclusions are simple.

All in all, it is recognized how very great a part nutrition plays in the life of cats. It conditions the development of kittens and their resistance to microbe diseases. In adults it can interpose in maladies due to mineral precipitates (vesical cases in particular) and in female sterility.

The advice I should here like to offer I shall base on these various works.

We had better be logical about this: no leopard or tiger has ever preferred the most appetizing roast to the fresh, raw meat of his victim. The cat is much too close to his savage cousins not to share instinctively these tastes.

So we can admit as a first principle the importance of raw food.

Raw food it must be, if one wants the female to be prolific. In this case, observation confirms the experiments: females who just eat cooked food produce only a small number of off-spring and often die while giving birth. Similarly, over-cooked foods result in nervous disorders, in constitutional troubles, irregularities in the formation of teeth and bones. The calcium metabolism is always more or less impaired, and a strain will rarely survive such a feeding method beyond the third generation.

If you doubt this, try feeding a kitten from weaning to the age of six months on the leavings from your cooking pots. In the event, even though you subsequently give him raw meat, fresh bones, thyroid extract, adrenalin and all possible vita-mins, you will never be able to bring him back to normal.

Submit an adult female to a regime of cooked foods for eighteen months, and she will require at least three years of raw rations before being able to give birth to normal offspring.

Because food gives life, those animals thoughtlessly fed on boiled meat and stews produce listless cats, hypothyroid types with generally retarded or deprived functions; short, rachitic kittens continually constipated; all those whom the most cursory pity would wish to put out of their misery, and for whom the most enlightened upbringing can do nothing.

Not to mention the grave lesions that laboratory tests show later: oedema, pulmonary atelectasis, osteoporosis, etc., also, under histological examination of the organs, showing up the errors committed because a cat is not a duck or even a delicate Pekingese.

A single meal, given in the evening, appears to me the best method of instituting a simple, ready routine and habit, provided that the meal be sufficient in quantity and quality.

Neither cold nor hot. Despite the miaowings of impatience, serve the food tepid. If it is too warm, wait for it to cool off. Over-cold food is not in order either. Thirsty as the cat may be in summer, never give him ice-cold milk direct from the refrigerator.

What meat? Beef or mutton are always all right. Not much horse-meat. Never offal, except heart, which, of course, is a muscle.

Grilled meat or boiled fish should be given in the quantity of one-quarter to one-third of a pound, to be increased or diminished according to the circumstances, the appetite and the 'figure' of the cat. You should add to this a dab of butter and some vegetables, preferably raw ones, such as grated carrots or salad. Leeks, asparagus, which cats adore, and cooked endive are excellent cleansers of the stomach and intestines, which so often are blocked with hairs which the cat swallows while washing himself.

Eggs, cheese, fresh cream, given twice a week in small quantities, constitute an excellent supplement of lecithin, vitamins, fats, calcium, etc. In principle, starches should be avoided; but do not fail to let him have a pot of grass (or papyrus) to which he will know instinctively to have recourse whenever necessary.

Last of all, do not forget that cats drink; but remember that milk is not very good for colitis, and that nothing can replace fresh, pure water, changed twice a day: simply water from the tap.

16. IF YOUR CAT
IS A FEMALE

If you have chosen and bought a pedigree cat, the chances are even that it is a male. But if you have got it from some friend it is almost sure to be a female. All the cats that one finds or are given are females. Perhaps because nature is less sparing of females than of males when a race is threatened. (It is the characteristic of poor and undernourished countries to be prolific in this way.)

Perhaps also because the poor little females 'on heat' who cry their desire on the empty air have more need of human tenderness than the prosaic toms do. Perhaps, lastly, because their masters, fed up with listening to them, have put them out on the streets.

However that may be, you are almost sure to find yourself with a queen. And the problem is urgent; whether, as she is a cat of quality, you want to have beautiful kittens from her; or pedigree or not, she will not wait for your permission to find herself a mate. In this latter case, the die is cast. In the former, calling for more definite action, where are you to find a mate worthy of her?

The various Cat Clubs, to be found all over the country, may be able to help you.

The rest is a question of correspondence, agreements,

differing conditions, that it is up to you to settle.

One single peculiarity of the 'feline proprieties': it is the female, as the more interested party, who does the travelling: it is she who has to go to the tom.

She should be taken in a closed basket, or one of those little carrying boxes to be obtained in pet-shops.

When she has reached her destination, the couple should not be left alone too precipitately. The absence of competitors eliminating the male's amorous jousting and leaving the female no time to prepare for his assault, there can be regrettable accidents owing to the male's roughness or the female's terror. Be cautious.

This meeting done with, here is some practical information for the days to come.

GESTATION

The queen 'carries' on the average for sixty-two days. Some cats may give birth from the sixty-fourth to the sixty-sixth, at the outermost. During that entire period, give the future mother a choice diet, richer in meat, eggs and fish than usually. It is a good thing too every morning to give her, mixed in sweetened condensed milk, six to eight drops of an essence of vitamins A and D, found in most chemists. Certain informed breeders will add an ounce of penicillin or aureomycin powder, the use of which has become current practice in the feeding of *bovidae* (milch cows or calves to be fattened).

Allowances must also be made for the expectant mother's behaviour. There are some who, in an advanced stage of gestation, cannot resist the need to steal a little extra meat or to take too personal an interest in the caged birds or the fish in the tank, which up to now they have always left in peace. They should not be punished for these thefts, which are no more than 'pregnant cravings'.

Queens who eat soap or who lick the bottom of the frying pan are not behaving any differently from women who demand a camembert at three in the morning.

In the latter half of the second month, the future mother

should not be let into the garden, if accidents are to be avoided and that instinct which all felines have of looking for a secret corner in which to hide their young is not to be aroused.

In the last week preceding the birth, one should keep watch to see that the natural functions are regular. In case of constipation, loss of appetite or keen thirst, a visit to the vet is in order. Even just the taking of her temperature can be valuable, since, apart from any pathological significance, in the last twenty-four hours, as it happens, the normal (which is approximately 101·5°) falls abruptly by one degree. Below 100·2° the arrival of the kittens is imminent.

Very conveniently set out by P. M. Soderberg in *Cat Breeding*, the following tables enable one to predict the date of birth within a few hours, when one knows the date of mating, and except when there are obstetric complications. In cases where these chronological calculations are gone beyond, it is essential to call in a vet.

CALENDAR OF FELINE PREGNANCIES
AND THE DATES OF GIVING BIRTH

January

Mating	1	2	3	4	5	6	7	8	9	10	11	12	13	14	15	16
Birth	7	8	9	10	11	12	13	14	15	16	17	18	19	20	21	22

March

January

Mating	17	18	19	20	21	22	23	24	25	26	27	28	29	30	31
Birth	23	24	25	26	27	28	29	30	31	1	2	3	4	5	6

March   April

February

Mating	1	2	3	4	5	6	7	8	9	10	11	12	13	14
Birth	7	8	9	10	11	12	13	14	15	16	17	18	19	20

April

February

Mating	15	16	17	18	19	20	21	22	23	24	25	26	27	28
Birth	21	22	23	24	25	26	27	28	29	30	1	2	3	4

April   May

March

Mating	1	2	3	4	5	6	7	8	9	10	11	12	13	14	15	16
Birth	5	6	7	8	9	10	11	12	13	14	15	16	17	18	19	20

May

March

Mating	17	18	19	20	21	22	23	24	25	26	27	28	29	30	31
Birth	21	22	23	24	25	26	27	28	29	30	31	1	2	3	4

May   June

April

Mating	1	2	3	4	5	6	7	8	9	10	11	12	13	14	15
Birth	5	6	7	8	9	10	11	12	13	14	15	16	17	18	19

June

Mating	16	17	18	19	20	21	22	23	24	25	26	27	28	29	30
Birth	20	21	22	23	24	25	26	27	28	29	30	1	2	3	4

June   July

May

Mating	1	2	3	4	5	6	7	8	9	10	11	12	13	14	15	16
Birth	5	6	7	8	9	10	11	12	13	14	15	16	17	18	19	20

July

May

Mating	17	18	19	20	21	22	23	24	25	26	27	28	29	30	31
Birth	21	22	23	24	25	26	27	28	29	30	31	1	2	3	4

July   August

June

Mating	1	2	3	4	5	6	7	8	9	10	11	12	13	14	15
Birth	5	6	7	8	9	10	11	12	13	14	15	16	17	18	19

August

June

Mating	16	17	18	19	20	21	22	23	24	25	26	27	28	29	30
Birth	20	21	22	23	24	25	26	27	28	29	30	31	1	2	3

August   September

Mating	1	2	3	4	5	6	7	8	9	10	11	12	13	14	15	16
Birth	4	5	6	7	8	9	10	11	12	13	14	15	16	17	18	19

September

Mating	17	18	19	20	21	22	23	24	25	26	27	28	29	30	31
Birth	20	21	22	23	24	25	26	27	28	29	30	1	2	3	4

September   October

August

Mating	1	2	3	4	5	6	7	8	9	10	11	12	13	14	15	16
Birth	5	6	7	8	9	10	11	12	13	14	15	16	17	18	19	20

October

August

Mating	17	18	19	20	21	22	23	24	25	26	27	28	29	30	31
Birth	21	22	23	24	25	26	27	28	29	30	31	1	2	3	4

October   November

September

Mating	1	2	3	4	5	6	7	8	9	10	11	12	13	14	15
Birth	5	6	7	8	9	10	11	12	13	14	15	16	17	18	19

November

September

Mating	16	17	18	19	20	21	22	23	24	25	26	27	28	29	30
Birth	20	21	22	23	24	25	26	27	28	29	30	1	2	3	4

November   December

October

Mating	1	2	3	4	5	6	7	8	9	10	11	12	13	14	15	16
Birth	5	6	7	8	9	10	11	12	13	14	15	16	17	18	19	20

December

October

Mating	17	18	19	20	21	22	23	24	25	26	27	28	29	30	31
Birth	21	22	23	24	25	26	27	28	29	30	31	1	2	3	4

December   January

November

Mating	1	2	3	4	5	6	7	8	9	10	11	12	13	14	15
Birth	5	6	7	8	9	10	11	12	13	14	15	16	17	18	19

January

November

Mating	16	17	18	19	20	21	22	23	24	25	26	27	28	29	30
Birth	20	21	22	23	24	25	26	27	28	29	30	31	1	2	3

January   February

Mating	1	2	3	4	5	6	7	8	9	10	11	12	13	14	15	16
Birth	4	5	6	7	8	9	10	11	12	13	14	15	16	17	18	19

February

December

Mating	17	18	19	20	21	22	23	24	25	26	27	28	29	30	31
Birth	20	21	22	23	24	25	26	27	28	1	2	3	4	5	6

February   March

The use of these tables is very simple. It is sufficient to note the day of mating, and to read immediately below, in the corresponding square, the almost certain date on which the cat will give birth.

THE BIRTH

There was a time when the birth, far from being a subject of unease or complications, was waited and wished for like a sort of victory. The Egyptians worshipped the female cat, in her time of gestation, under the name of 'Lady of Heaven'. They dedicated their own new-born to her, hanging round a baby's neck a medallion bearing the effigy of the goddess Bast with a cat's head.

More prosaically, today we content ourselves with giving females in kitten the true comfort that they require. Avoid over-soft cushions and those over-padded nests prepared in ignorance and love. The most delicate cat will prefer the bare floor, an old carpet, above all an enclosed box, to these luxuries.

Just place a lining of rubber at the bottom of any old box four feet long by one and a half or two feet high, and provide – as the final attention – a curtain.

Then leave her to it. Apart from exceptional cases (and better to leave these to a vet rather than to the cleverest amateur) nature has so equipped the mother, that everything should pass off very smoothly.

First the 'waters break'; then at the rate of a birth every quarter of an hour on average, the little cats are expelled in the course of two or three contractions. In between times, the mother licks them all over, and under this rough scraper the new-born rapidly take on the appearance of woolly chicks with tight-shut eyes (they will remain blind for ten days), which makes them, whether they be Abyssinians or alley-cats, the most disarming little creatures in the world.

If the cord, which has linked them up to now to that feeding and heating station that is the mother, is badly severed and too long, don't hesitate. Cut it off under one half-inch from the stomach and disinfect immediately, dabbing the little wound with alcohol or iodine.

When with the arrival of the fourth or fifth baby (in rare cases, the sixth), you have the impression that it is all over, take care not to try to set everything to rights. Nature will take care of this far better than you.

Let the mother make sure that she runs no more risk. If she seems worn out, let her get her breath, let her rest for an hour, then give her a good meal. Certain breeders advocate in such cases a saucer of sugared milk in which two raw eggs have been mixed. Others have more success with offering seven ounces of minced meat, just barely warmed.

If she eats, everything is all right.

Should she turn up her nose at the meal and take only liquid, call the vet. A bad delivery, or a belated afterbirth – and on his energetic intervention or your guilty negligence depends all the future.

THE KITTENS

If the cat has sufficient milk to feed her entire litter, the little ones will grow bigger from day to day, and the progress recorded will be rapid.

At ten days the kittens will open their eyes and squint a little.

At twelve days, sounds will seem to intrigue them; the ear is growing and uncurling. Even as soon as this some will purr.

At fifteen days the eyes will be clear blue and their gaze full of wonder.

At twenty-two days, sturdier ones, rejoicing in their first teeth, will try their first steps out of the box.

A month passes away, and the purity of the little cats passes away too. And you notice for the first time what until then the mother had cleaned up promptly with an efficient tongue.

Each one takes on his own responsibilities, and although the maternal 'feeding station' still finds the kittens just as eager, intent, and greedy to the point of going to sleep on the spot rather than give up their place, already from this day forward it should be possible to wean them, letting them alternate their suckling with substantial cereals.

Thereafter their appetites grow daily more exacting. Soon the cereals no longer suffice. The mother with her drained teats gets away from these tyrants who harass and lacerate her.

From the forty-fifth day, especially in large litters, it is essential to curb their selfish eagerness, if the mother is to be protected from the rigours of eclampsia, which occurs more frequently than is generally believed when nursing goes on for too long.

WEANING

After two months it is best to proceed to weaning. One morning give the cat a purging on an empty stomach with a dose of castor oil, after having separated her once for all from her young.

For the future the latter should receive a concentrated oil preparation of vitamins which previously the mother had drunk. Three or four drops a day will suffice for each kitten for one or two months.

Their individual dishes (one should avoid communal meals, in which the timid ones do badly), filled twice a day, at noon and five p.m., should contain a little pulpy meat, raw or slightly cooked, or some crumbed fish without bones, or else some grated carrot mixed with yolk of egg, and, according to the consistency of their stools, rice or mashed noodles.

Independently of these two good meals, a breakfast of condensed milk or a cereal mush, given each morning at eight, will always be acceptable.

EDUCATION OF THE YOUNG

The weaning accomplished, leave things to the mother. No other female, as it happens, has a greater sense of her authority and duties in the matter. No other female knows better just when and how to administer a timely cuff with the paw or the soothing comfort of a lick to set the naughty ones straight.

I cannot resist including this extract, on the subject of maternal instruction, from a letter I received from one of my correspondents:

'One of my cats', wrote Mme H. Viollet, 'gave a special upbringing to one kitten, an only son very advanced for his age and who already, at six weeks, was aspiring to share the adults' meals. One morning the mother appeared holding a live mouse between her teeth. The inquisitive kitten approached, then started away frightened. Whereupon the cat, doubtless to reassure him, began a strange game: she let go of her prey, caught it at the slightest impulse to flight, only to let it go again immediately; and the merry-go-round continued like this until the little cat, emboldened and won over by her example, took up in turn the same cruel game. Then the mother, having no doubt thought the demonstration enough, swiftly broke the mouse's back and ate it up, under the astonished eyes of the little onlooker.

'The next day she brought a dead bird, put it down in front of her son, and began to encourage him, as she had done on the previous day. Every time she would accompany her expressive miming with the onomatopoeia: "Baniananay! Baniananay!" which, in all probability, means in cat language, "Come on quickly! Quickly!"; and the kitten, remembering the feast of yesterday's mouse enjoyed by his mother, began to devour the little bird, of which he left only the skull.

'I took the untouched head that he had left,' Mme Viollet went on, 'and laid it in front of the cat, who was watching from very nearby. Extremely dignified, she turned away from it. I persisted; she got up and went to sit at a little distance, accompanied by her kitten, who followed her with a quiet step. Tired of all these fine airs, I moved away, but without taking my eyes off the two ruffians. Then delicately the cat took up the remainder of the bird between her jaws and brought it to the kitten, repeating to him several times, "Baniananay! Baniananay!" "Come on, quickly! Quickly!" And the kitten, his eyes half-closed and looking thoroughly nauseated, came to a decision. He bit into that skull, at first without enthusiasm, then with pleasure, and crunched it, while his mother's eyes sparkled with pride and joy.'

Setting aside the anthropomorphism, is it not splendidly observed, this gastronomic lesson? Certainly all mothers behave in a similar fashion, all show this same pride in the warranted sacrifice, in the initiation and the progress that marks it; but here it was a question of a female cat, and the eloquence and mimicry are memorable indeed. The cat world is not prodigal of these qualities.

Later there will be the conflicts, the jealousies, misunderstandings and disputes. Afterwards will come the games, mock struggles, comic battles, the concessions, the seizing of power and the joint agreements: an entire succession of events, requirements and responses in various activities, a whole common behaviour pattern which will gradually replace the individual spirit with the 'clan' spirit, with all its deputies, chiefs, representatives and laws: a living theatre, with a hundred different acts, which one watches with feelings that vary between admiration and annoyance, but which, without one's knowing it, holds one in a delightful bondage.

Forewarned is forearmed.

If you let three months pass, if you let opportunities slip by, if you don't take advantage of your friends' admiration at exactly the right second, if you hesitate about putting one of these delightful little tyrants into their arms (provided they are worthy), your course is beyond recall, and your regrets useless.

You had a single cat at the beginning of this chapter. From now on, you will have six.

But if you are not a breeder. If you don't happen to be under their spell. If, for a variety of reasons, among which at random may be cited the strong odour of the male, the concert-parties of the amorous female, your valuable stuffs and furniture, concern for public opinion, and a grander unwillingness not to have to pronounce sentence of death one day. If, for some of these reasons, you prefer not to expose yourself to the unforeseen consequences of maternity and if you have decided, wrongly or rightly, to deprive your cat of her prerogatives, it is certainly essential for you to learn about the means at your disposal for practising this birth control without remorse or regret.

CASTRATION

If, living in a town, one owns only one cat, castration is established as inevitable.

To keep a stallion in a flat is to condemn him to boredom, to celibacy. Allowing him to get away, to answer the call of the female living opposite, is to risk losing him or seeing him return scabby, injured and dirty (and these are the lesser ills of liberty regained).

For a tom by himself, except in the country perhaps, castration is thus a necessity.

One should not wait more than five or six months to go ahead with this very simple surgical intervention. The operation involves no aftermath, no deplorable pain, if it is performed by a vet, and under the indispensable anaesthesia.

The consequences are not, as so widely believed, apathy, obesity, indifference. Castrated toms are almost all as playful, affectionate, intelligent, as any others. Only those who are over-fed turn into those heavy, sleepy puddings who don't need to be eunuchs to be overburdened with fat and threatened with congestion.

Is it a bad moment for the tom to get through? Hardly, since he has no apprehensions, no pre-operational anguish; and on coming round, he remembers nothing. Afterwards, there is the secure calm of life without passion or drama.

An existence which many wise men might well choose, if it were possible completely to forget and renounce everything, including the memory itself of desire.

To deprive a female cat of all sexual activity is a graver undertaking. The removal of the ovaries (or ovariotomy) entails a serious surgical operation with laparotomy and deep general anaesthesia. However, this operation is now commonly practised by all the specialists, and thanks to antibiotics no longer offers the danger that formerly had to be reckoned with.

We must refrain from sentimentality in discussing as a matter of principle the suitability of an operation which is often performed for grave pathological reasons. Compared with other females, cats have a highly-strung temperament, as we have seen. Moreover, they are frequently affected with cysts of the ovary, uterine hyperplasia and various glandular malfunctionings; and the exacerbated temperament then becomes a source of irritation to everyone about them.

Only surgery holds the key to these troubles, and it is hardly a matter of 'not loving cats' or defying 'nature's simple laws' if we want to safeguard and relieve them when we can.

17. AILMENTS

There is a system of surgery for the cat. Not only that surgery of convenience to which we have just alluded, but a day-to-day surgery: that to deal with gastro-intestinal accidents (cats, much more circumspect than dogs, are less exposed to the risks of gustative curiosity); foreign bodies in the mouth (a needle treacherously broken in the tongue or pharynx, or else a bone wedged between the dental arcades); difficulties in maternity and uterine infections; lastly, traumatism (fractures, lacerations, sores, varying injuries following a serious fall from the fifth floor or the encounter with a car which they have not been able to dodge).

This survey has developed side by side with canine surgery, which, drawing its inspiration increasingly from the art of human surgery, has profited from the advances made in the latter.

Cat medicine is relatively of much more recent date: Why? Simply because the sick cat is reserved.

THE CAT IS NEVER 'SICK AS A DOG'

The cat does not complain. The female accomplishes her labour in silence, and the male is not a whiner. In the face of suffering both have – resignation or scorn? – an overwhelming dignity. When the cat stops eating, has a thirst and can drink no more; when he refuses all food for more than a day, he is neither unhappy nor sulking: he is ill.

It is not a matter here of writing on this subject a *vade mecum* summary of feline therapeutics, but simply of drawing attention to this important point of cat symptomatology: *the sick cat is reserved*.

So then, don't wait for him to be dying before having him seen to.

Don't wait for him to cough, spit, sniffle and give way to the demonstrations by which a dog usually betrays its mild indisposition.

Don't wait for him to utter heart-breaking signs, or to roll his eyes tragically by way of telling you, as the dog does, 'My throat is burning,' or else, 'I am choking.' The cat has far too much modesty, pride and self-respect.

He settles warily into his shivers, his respiratory trouble or his stomach pain, and waits.

Add to this the fact that, hypersensitive to the unaccustomed, to strange places, every cat is by nature suspicious of people who are not 'his'. If you know that the least unusual gesture is suspect to him, that the gentlest examination appears an act of hostility, the least insistent solicitude a threat, you will understand why this branch of animal medicine has marked time.

Certainly, given a little experience, one succeeds in examining and treating such patients without too much difficulty, but it is in the laboratory rather than in the clinic that feline pathology has progressed.

Need one give some examples?

Before the war, we knew – just – about only two severe infectious diseases, both of which developed with great rapidity. Three days, or four at the most, and the cat was either cured or had succumbed to what was then called infectious-influenza, if the predominant symptoms were respiratory; or typhus, if they were of a digestive kind.

Since then, important research has enabled us to differentiate the pathogenic agent responsible; we have been able to subdivide these diseases into morbid entities and put at the disposal of practitioners effective vaccines. In the meantime, other serious ailments have been brought to light, such as leucopenia, leptospirosis, piroplasmosis; and, following sulphonamides, the arsenal of therapeutics, enriched by antibiotics, provides sufficient weapons for speedy conquest.

Has there thus been established between cats and their doctors a gradual process of getting used to each other? Our taloned patients seem to adapt themselves a little more easily to treatment. On both sides the examination and, if it is necessary, surgical intervention, take place without so much apprehension.

For several years now cats have been less fierce when they pay a visit to their doctor. Temperature-taking upsets only novices. Females having trouble with their delivery submit to the forceps. Subcutaneous injections are borne without too much fuss, and old cats who have urethral stones know perfectly well that they must submit without flinching to the delicate probings which always bring liberating relief to their vain efforts.

CARES THAT YOU CAN TAKE

In the cat, as I have said, microbes and viruses rarely give way when treatment is too long delayed. It is better to have a false alarm than to have to hear that little phrase: 'It is too late.'

Acute infection in the cat in fact often takes so violent, so rapid, a form that the uninformed immediately think of accident or malevolence: 'Our cat has been poisoned.'

And so he has been, but by a killing virus which the vet can only combat if you go to see him in time.

At the first abnormal symptom, therefore, take the cat's temperature.

The temperature of a cat, like that of a dog, fluctuates between 101° and 101·6°. Beyond 102·6° the alarm is always serious. But you must know that on the other hand when it falls to 99·5° it is more dangerous still.

Where to take it? Not under the arm nor in the groin, and of course not in the mouth. Slightly anoint the tip of the thermometer with Vaseline or cold cream and hold both the instrument and the cat's tail with the same hand. There is no better way of keeping hold of both.

HOW TO EXAMINE THE THROAT

Examination of the mouth and the various investigations that a vet carries out on a cat whom he is probably seeing for the first time, always give rise to some wondering astonishment, if not anxiety.

'Goodness! You're not really afraid of being bitten?'

Certainly not. It is rare for one to be bitten when one opens that little pink mouth, adorned with sharp and pointed teeth. The mere audacity of this gesture (if it is done calmly and deliberately) impresses and intimidates the patient. It is therefore preferable to consult a vet in his surgery rather than to ask him to come and see your invalid at home.

To open a cat's mouth a minimum of steadiness and gentleness should suffice. The left hand grips the head firmly from behind, with the whole palm, while the thumb and middle finger tighten slightly against the cheeks so as to keep the jaws half-open. The index-finger of the right hand then presses lightly on the tongue to reveal the back of the throat.

If the throat is normal, the amygdalae should not be visible, and the soft palate should not be streaked with those red arborescences which are the little, congested vessels.

In cases of inflammation, one should begin at all events by anointing with the help of a brush (never with a long-handled swab of cotton-wool) soaked in an antiseptic collutorium, and one should wrap the neck with cotton or wool while waiting for the opinion of a specialist.

HOW TO MAKE A CAT SWALLOW A PILL

An identical technique will enable you to make a cat swallow a small pill without difficulty. The head held always with the left hand, one drops the pill at the base of the tongue, and at that very second one lets go of the patient's head, clapping the hands swiftly. The reflex triggered off by this noise, as simultaneous as unexpected, causes a swallowing motion, and the pill goes down.

HOW TO ADMINISTER A LIQUID

Whatever the liquid is, one should use a large dropper with blunt edges, and get the cat to drink *without trying to open his jaws*. The little glass tube placed at the juncture of the two lips must leave free all movement of the lower jaw and permit the closing of the mouth. Without this precaution, swallowing is not possible.

How many people persist, however, in trying to make a cat swallow liquid with his mouth open! Try yourself to swallow your saliva without closing your lips. Then you will understand.

HOW TO GIVE AN ENEMA OR
INTRODUCE A SUPPOSITORY

There are not ten ways, especially if one is alone: the cat, wrapped in a covering and placed on the table, is held without force under the left arm. The left hand lifts up the tail, while the right operates, with the least possible hesitation. Cats generally utter a great cry, then seem to make the best of such a humiliation and let themselves be treated.

In the case of an enema, one imagines that some mysterious

instinct of imminent relief dictates their ultimate surrender.

As for suppositories, in view of the difficulties that attend the oral administration of many disagreeable medicaments, they constitute for the cat the most rapid as well as the most effective method of reception, and for the vet or owner the minimum of rebellion to fear.

HOW TO GIVE A SUBCUTANEOUS INJECTION

Injections (subcutaneous, intradermic or intravenous) are commonly used in veterinary medicine because they have the advantage of enabling the immediate administration of medicaments that are concentrated or taste unpleasant. One can understand then why feline medicine uses this therapeutic method more than any other.

Intravenous or intramuscular injections are too delicate an operation for me to give their technique here. It is essential, on the other hand, for every cat-lover to be able to administer a simple injection under the skin. In cases of haemorrhage or syncope, on the speed of this intervention, in the absence of a vet, can depend the ultimate chance of salvation.

The syringe, first taken to pieces (body and sucker separated) should be placed in cold water and then sterilized by bringing to the boil, together with the needle, for several minutes. Once charged with the medicine to be injected, the syringe is ready for the operation. This latter can be performed directly, the needle fixed securely in the instrument, or else in two stages, first inserting the needle, which one then joins to the syringe.

The cat's conjunctive tissue is rich enough for one to be able to choose any place in the body (back, shoulder, inner side of the thighs, etc.), but the place most easily accessible is the base of the neck at shoulder-height.

If you have taken the precaution of disinfecting the skin with a little alcohol or ether, and if you have not dirtied the needle, this little operation should not be followed by any septic complications.

* * * *

Such is the minimum knowledge necessary in order to bestow the attentions of current veterinary practice.

And never forget that cats are, more than children, frightened and sensitive beings. Speak to them to reassure them.

Speak to them, even if they do not seem to listen or to hear you.

And be quiet in your movements. Calmness is catching.

SYMPTOMS THAT YOU SHOULD RECOGNIZE

One does not learn medicine only in books. One does not only become a doctor by empiricism. These pages, therefore, have no other aim than to give the beginner general indications of proved symptoms, while underlining their importance where it is necessary.

DIGESTIVE TROUBLES

In the cat's pathology, digestive signs are the more eloquent because the cat is not a ruminant. He tears his food, as we have seen, rends it, mashing it somewhat in the process, and swallows it down at one go. He eats very fast, but vomits easily and has a delicate intestinal tract.

Many reasons why digestive troubles are the first to attract the attention of the indifferent or the uninformed.

What importance are we to give them?

That kitten who was playing with a threaded needle found on the ground, begins suddenly to salivate or to cry, the needle driven into his throat. That tom making desperate efforts to get out a flat bone, a cartilaginous fragment or some rubbish stuck in his jaws. And that other vomits up some worms or some matted hair which he has been harbouring for several weeks.

None of these varied signs is accompanied by fever if his life is not in danger. But should the thermometer stand at or pass 102·2°, should the tongue appear burnt at its tip as if by an acid, should the cat, prostrated, depressed, remain with his nose in his milk without lapping up the least drop; these are the occasions for alarm. It is no longer a question of an accident, but of a very grave illness: typhus, with which certain animals severely affected sometimes die in a few hours.

RESPIRATORY AFFECTIONS

These troubles, in general less obvious, do none the less betray a serious condition.

The nose is running? The cat sneezes? Temperature! It is an infectious coryza which is far from being a simple cold; it is a microbe rhinitis which one must hasten to check.

The cat is coughing? Temperature! If the temperature climbs to 102·2° to 104°, if he is short of breath, if, with his paws tucked in, he remains immobile and stiff, one can be almost certain that the bronchitis is complicated by a severe pneumonia, which can develop rapidly and dramatically.

AFFECTIONS OF THE CIRCULATORY SYSTEM AND OF THE BLOOD

They are relatively rare (I am speaking of real cardiac complaints), but one can be anxious about anaemia betrayed by pale mucous membranes, discoloured gums, associated with frequent drowsiness, melancholy, wasting. It corresponds very often to an affection of the blood, of parasitic origin, which cats who go free in gardens or the country contract for the same reason as dogs do: it is the piroplasmosis with which hunting men are well acquainted and, on the Mediterranean coast, leishmaniasis, less spectacular initially but far graver.

It is by affections of the blood likewise, accompanied or not by digestive troubles, that is manifested an ailment that has been discovered comparatively recently: infectious leucopenia. Long disregarded, this veritable scourge of the cat has accounted for up to 95 per cent of the victims that were believed to have been affected by typhus, and who were treated in vain by sulphonamides, which have no effect on this virus.

Only a strong preventive vaccination can protect cats from this terrible disease, and only some known antibiotics effectively help to combat it, if the blood test has given confirmation of a clinical diagnosis which remains hard to make because the disease is attended by imprecise symptoms.

SKIN TROUBLES

Itching, falling hair and often scabs and scales cannot long go unnoticed.

Mycosis? Mange? Eczema? Only the vet can tell by proceeding if necessary to a microscopic examination. Here, too, prevention is better than cure, and early is better than late.

The first of these two pointers teaches the avoidance of contagion (by frequenting unknown cats or communal games with cats in the country) when it is a question of fungoid dermatitis or parasites.

The second advises surveillance of the diet and general functioning, if it is a question of sores in which all possibility of contagion can be ruled out.

Nevertheless, one should not neglect the irritant effect of fleas and other external parasites in cats left to themselves or where the bodily hygiene is not attended to.

There remains finally ear mange, so widespread and common, to which many owners who in other respects take great care of their cats pay little heed. They are wrong. The affection, at the outset pruriginous and merely disagreeable, often has complications of head mange, very quickly spread and practically incurable, or even of serious otitis, source of meningitis.

LOCOMOTORY TROUBLES

One would have to be quite unfeeling towards cats not to notice when one is dragging his paw as he walks, another refraining from jumping on to the furniture, or a third protecting from every movement a suddenly painful limb.

The least examination frightens him? He spits his indignation or fear as soon as one barely touches him? It is a possible fracture, for the cat is really cowardly only in such a case.

He lends himself without too much trouble to tender curiosity, understands your solicitude? It is a question of a simple accident: injury, wound or abscess.

You must know, however, that there are five toes on the front paws, of which only four are for support, of which four claws only are used and are shortened by roofing or walking but that the claw of the thumb continues to grow and, in cats confined to the house, becomes ingrown more often than one would imagine.

Lastly, is your cat old, too well-fed, or sedentary? Time then to think of rheumatism and arthritis, before they become chronic.

EYE TROUBLES

The cat's marvellously beautiful eyes reveal his manifold states of feeling. They are also very vulnerable mirrors of his health.

Watering, eyelids half-closed, mark the first warning symptoms: conjunctivitis or blepharitis, and sometimes the very painful presence of an unsuspected foreign body.

Moreover, we should not take lightly the white or grey shading, nor the more or less opalescent film of corneal ailments; and still less, as little obvious as it may be, a deep, unilateral haemorrhage: it is, alas, in the majority of cases an attack of a serious infection dreaded by veterinary surgeons and breeders; tuberculosis of the eye.

GENITAL AND URINARY COMPLAINTS

Two groups of distinct symptoms, but it seems more in order to assemble them under one heading, so as to popularize practical observation of them.

Genital symptoms: metritis always suggested by a stomach abnormally swollen, pain on palpation, an evident lack of appetite, a fever . . . and still more when a discharge, even a trivial one, soils the vulva and the bed of the invalid.

Signs indirectly genital are all swellings, tumours, and any hardening of the mammaries.

Urinary troubles, on the other hand, are indicated by insufficient urination, which is the eloquent sign of cystitis and nephritis, and the vain efforts on the sanitary tray for the difficult emission of more or less bloody urine indicating the presence of stones, more common among castrated cats than among any other mammals in the world.

Why? The opinions of the best clinical physicians differ on this point; but there is no space here for discussions of this kind, in which we had better not get ourselves involved.

The roll of 'his ailments' has aimed only at accenting general symptoms that it is essential to know; since the cat himself disdains to shed light on them.

And this last detail of his behaviour still remains a disturbing mystery.

One would say that the cat no longer expects anything, from life or from people. He is the prisoner of time.

Humanity, more than a little mad, as it must seem to him, with its fussing, chattering and gesticulating around him, he knows well.

He has long since judged and understood it: and he submits to it.

Does he remember that he was once a god, and more feared than a king? That he used to be, at the hour of his death, more surrounded, more venerated than a prince?

And the cat who dies today, does he simply expect to be given the same veneration, to have the same words spoken to him, and the same gestures made him as formerly, in Egypt? Who can tell?

> 'I will not reign,
> To serve I disdain,
> The cat I remain!'

This doggerel might well be the motto of this fabulous creature of whom nothing is known, almost nothing, unless that of all the animals on the earth he is the only one mid-way between the domestic animal and that called wild, and the only one who, through happy and unhappy times, has never done other than his own sweet will.

THE EAGLE AND THE DOVE
A Study in Contrasts: Saint Teresa of Avila – Saint Thérèse of Lisieux
V. Sackville-West

Two women, both destined to be revered as saints; but how very different they were in character, opinions and life-style is lucidly conveyed in this exceptional double biography from the pen of the redoubtable V. Sackville-West.

'I have nothing but admiration for a brilliant and sensitive piece of writing' – V. S. Pritchett

Biography/History 40p

THE PREFECT STRANGER
P. J. Kavanagh

This celebrated autobiography, winner of the Richard Hillary Memorial Prize for 1966, is as readable and funny as it is hauntingly tender. It is P. J. Kavanagh's tribute to the memory of his first wife, Sally, the perfect stranger – and it is also the absorbing, amusing tale of his early years, from his schooldays and undergraduate life to the time he spent in Korea as a soldier and his happy, but short-lived, marriage to Sally.

'A real book; human, tender, gentle, loving, intelligent' – *Sheffield Morning Telegraph*

'A love story beautifully told' – *Sunday Telegraph*

Autobiography 40p

AN ORKNEY TAPESTRY
George Mackay Brown
with drawings by Sylvia Wishart

George Mackay Brown is one of Scotland's most gifted poets and short story writers, whose work is universally acclaimed. He lives in Stromness, where he has always lived. *An Orkney Tapestry* is his testimonial to his native land, a celebration of the roots of a community which mixes history, legend, drama and folklore into a rich and varied tapestry.

'George Mackay Brown is a portent. No one else writes like this or has this feeling for language . . . His is an innate talent: as true as that of Yeats' – Jo Grimond, *Spectator*

Literature/Travel 50p

These books are obtainable from booksellers and newsagents or can be ordered direct from the Publishers. Send a cheque or postal order for the purchase price plus 6p postage and packing to Quartet Books Limited, P.O. Box 11, Falmouth, Cornwall TR10 9EN.

The cat. Mysterious, secretive, unfathomable; neither tamed nor savage, capable of inspiring great fear and great love in human beings; a fabulous creature, with a terrible history of suffering.

In *Just Cats*, Fernand Méry – an internationally acknowledged expert on cats – comes as close as anyone ever has to shedding light on this dark and beautiful animal.

Here is history, legend and observation, a fund of knowledge spiced with fascinating stories and anecdotes about individual cats, and full of invaluable advice to cat owners on all aspects of caring for and breeding cats of every variety from the majestic Persian Blue to the dustbin-hunting Ginger Tabby.

Just Cats is just that: a unique manual to delight, inform and entertain every cat lover, complete with eight pages of superb photographs.

NATURAL HISTORY / REFERENCE

ISBN 0 704 31037 6

United Kingdom 50p
Canada $1.95   Australia* & New Zealand $1.65

Quartet

*Recommended price only